SMUGGLERS ALL

SMUGGLERS ALL

Centuries of Norfolk Smuggling

Kenneth Hipper

To our grandchildren,
Tristan and Eloise

The Larks Press

Published by the Larks Press
Ordnance Farmhouse
Guist Bottom, Dereham, Norfolk NR20 5PF
Tel/Fax 01328 829207

E-mail: Larks.Press@btinternet.com

Printed by the Lanceni Press, Garrood Drive, Fakenham.

First published October 2001
Reprinted June 2003

British Library Cataloguing-in-Publication Data.
A catalogue record for this book is available from the British Library.

COVER
The picture on the cover is a drawing by W.H.Pine, c. 1805,
coloured by David Yaxley.

The drawing on p.125 is by David Yaxley
All other drawings are by the author.

ISBN 1 904006 02 7

Acknowledgements

This book is the result of many years' research during which time I have received help from a number of people. I would like to thank the staff of the Norfolk Studies Library and Norfolk Record Office. I am also indebted to the late Dr Roger Virgoe for reading the text.

I am grateful to H. M. Customs and Excise, the Norfolk Studies Library and the late Michael Seago who have kindly given permission to use photographic illustrations.

Finally I would like to thank my daughter Susan for assistance with typing and Hilary, my wife, without whose encouragement and interest the book would not have been written.

Kenneth Hipper

CONTENTS

Introduction... 7
Glossary... 10
1. Export Smuggling in Early Times......................... 11
2. Growth of Import Smuggling............................ 24
3. Free Traders in Control................................ 46
4. Norwich and the Fair Traders........................... 61
5. The Conflict at Sea.................................... 72
6. The Preventive Waterguard and the Coastguard....... 89
7. Farming and Smuggling................................ 109
8. Public Attitudes to the Free Traders.................... 123
9. Regional Smuggling.................................... 134
10. Smuggling Tales...................................... 153
11. The Decline of Smuggling............................. 164
Bibliography..167
Index...169

**Sir Robert Walpole 1676–1745, Norfolk's most famous
customer of the smuggling trade.**

Introduction

People have always resented paying taxes of any kind, and many will go to great lengths to avoid paying them. For centuries people have taken the attitude that tax evasion is one of the lesser crimes. Such an attitude became evident throughout the country in the thirteenth century, when the Crown decided to raise revenue by imposing customs duties on a number of commodities, which included wool, woolfells, and hides. This led to these articles being smuggled out of the country on a large scale. As time passed the number of items on which duty had to be paid increased and the Crown had to introduce new laws to combat smuggling. Consequently more officials were appointed to enforce these laws. This book is an account of the part played by people in and around Norfolk, illegally exporting and importing goods, over a period of several centuries.

An outline account of the early period of export smuggling shows which goods were profitable and how they were smuggled out of Norfolk. Men who smuggled wool out of the county were known as 'owlers', probably because they went about their business at night. Commodities such as wool, on which export duties were charged, or the export of which was prohibited, were attractive to smugglers. Large profits were to be made by merchants, wool-growers and others who assisted them to smuggle their produce overseas. Later, Tudor corn laws were to make grain a profitable item to smuggle, and companies trading in textiles also suffered at the hands of smugglers. Since Norfolk was an agricultural county and had a flourishing textile industry, large quantities of goods were secretly transported overseas without customs duties being paid. An excise tax was introduced on many goods in the seventeenth century and this increased the scope of the smugglers as more items became profitable to smuggle.

Although this account is primarily concerned with smuggling in and out of Norfolk, the national and international scene has been considered, particularly the countries to which goods were smuggled in the early centuries of large-scale export smuggling. Also taken into account are the foreign ports where businesses were set up in support of the smuggling industry during the later centuries of import smuggling. County boundaries of course meant nothing to smuggling gangs, some of which came from the London area and Kent to smuggle their goods into the counties along the east coast. Many smuggling gangs included men from both Norfolk and Suffolk, and where necessary some smuggling activities have been included from Suffolk and other east coast areas.

In Norfolk, smuggling took place throughout the county. Contraband was supplied to customers in the yards and streets of Norwich, the county market towns, and the highways and byways of the remotest parts. Indeed some highways became major smuggling routes, like Smugglers' Road in Breckland.

Smuggling has been romanticised to such an extent that the truth has been obscured. The facts need no embellishment and provide enough drama in themselves.

Smuggling has many facets and hitherto writers seem to have concentrated primarily on sea smuggling, and what took place in coastal areas. This book attempts to give a balanced view of the smuggling industry from early times, mainly in Norfolk. It traces the growth of import smuggling and the struggle on land and at sea with the Revenue services.

The relationship between the industries of smuggling and agriculture has also been taken into account. In early times agriculture provided some of the most lucrative commodities to smuggle, such as wool and later grain. Import smuggling from the seventeenth to the nineteenth century was a labour-intensive occupation, requiring large numbers of men, horses, wagons and carts, many of which came from Norfolk farms. Farm buildings and land also provided temporary hiding places. The interdependence of these industries was much in evidence at this time, especially when the income from smuggling was greater than that derived from agriculture.

Surprisingly, economic historians have neglected the effect of smuggling on local industry and trade in Norwich, for so long one of the largest provincial cities. Manufacturers involved in the textile industry in both the city and the county were concerned about the effect of the illegal export of wool on their trade, and later there is evidence that vast amounts of contraband were smuggled into Norwich, making life very difficult for honest dealers in tea, gin and other commodities.

The public attitude towards the smugglers and contraband had a considerable effect on the profitability of smuggling. While the general public looked favourably on smuggling, or turned a blind eye, the smugglers could count on support, transport and assistance from local people when they needed it. This was also reflected in the courts by the light sentences meted out to smugglers. Later, when duties were reduced, the public did not have to rely on the smugglers for goods, and they became less sympathetic towards them. The courts were also not so lenient, and smugglers either went to prison or had to pay heavy fines.

A chapter has been devoted to smuggling tales, which have been taken from newspapers and books. These tales are likely to be true and have a useful part to play in showing some of the people who were involved in contraband running, and some of the ploys they used to escape detection.

The old coinage of pounds, shillings and pence has not been converted into modern decimal coinage, as the former bears no relation to the latter in terms of value: the eighteenth century 10s. was worth considerably more than the modern 50p.

The beach between Mundesley and Bacton.
Medieval owlers shipped wool overseas from here.

Glossary

Anker   A liquid measure formerly used in all areas trading with Holland. An anker tub had a capacity of 10 gallons (Winchester wine measure) before 1824 and 8⅓ imperial gallons after that date. Tubs shipped across the North Sea were not filled to capacity. For example half-ankers containing 3½ gallons of spirits were so much over-proof that an additional 2½ gallons of water would be added. The six gallons were then sold in England at a good profit.
It is possible that tubs were not filled to capacity in order to improve their buoyancy if they were to be thrown overboard.

Clove   Wool weight, 71 lbs.

Cocket   Certificate to show that duty has been paid.

Cohorn (Coehorn)   A small mortar for throwing grenades.

Collector   Senior customs officer at a main port or ports responsible to the Board of Customs.

Comptroller   Officer appointed by the Board of Customs to ensure that a correct return is made of the duties collected.

Dollop   There seems to be no standard weight for a dollop of tea; 13lbs., 28lbs. and 40lbs. are some weights suggested by historians. Bags of tea seized in Norfolk contained varying quantities. It is therefore more likely to be a name given to a bag or sack of tea, than a particular quantity.

Dragoon   A mounted soldier, armed with sword and carbine.

Gunlocks   Mechanism by which the charge of a gun is exploded.

Hanger   Short sword.

Hide   Animal skin, raw or dressed.

Nankeens   Trousers, named after Nanking in China where they were first made.

Stoup bottle   Capacity about 2 pints

Stuff   Woollen fabric.

Tamer (Teamer)   Waggon pulled by five horses.

The Nore   Naval district in which Chatham is located.

Tide-Surveyor   Preventive officer in charge of a boarding or rummage crew.

Tide-Waiter   A shore-based customs officer who boarded vessels when they arrived in port.

Woolfell   Skin of sheep with wool still on.

1. Export Smuggling in Early Times

In 1275 the first permanent staff of customs officials was established to collect export duties on wool at the ports. The coastline was divided into thirteen areas and a Custom House was built at the principal port in each area. Ships could not load, or unload, any goods at other ports or harbours without an official from the main port being present. In fact the duties were collected mainly at these ports and it was left to the discretion of the officials whether they kept watch on the other harbours and landing-places in their area. For example, the officials at Great Yarmouth were in charge of the coastline from Blakeney in Norfolk to Woodbridge in Suffolk.

As time passed, duty had to be paid on many other items; these included commodities imported as well as exported. A large number of ships were arrested at the ports throughout the country for not paying wine duties in 1326/7. At Great Yarmouth 39 ships were arrested and 14 were detained at Bishop's Lynn, which became King's Lynn in 1537.

In every port there was a 'tronour', whose job it was to weigh the wool on the 'tron', scales in the form of a beam. These scales were known as the King's Beam and were located outside every Custom House. Merchants had to pay a toll on their wool weighed in this way.

By 1332 smuggling was commonplace and Norfolk was one of a dozen counties where this was happening. The King was aware that collectors and controllers at the ports had allowed wool to be exported illegally, had taken bribes from merchants and allowed them to export their wool either unweighed or underweighed, thereby robbing the Crown of revenue.

The situation did not improve and in the 1340s the King was informed that unweighed wool and other goods were being exported by night and day from the east coast without payment of custom or subsidy. To combat this illegal trading, men were commissioned to search all vessels in the ports and other places along the coast, including rivers, or at sea between the ports. Two were commissioned to search the ports and freshwaters along the coast of Norfolk between, and including, Lynn and Great Yarmouth. They were to receive 10 % of the value of all the uncustomed goods they seized.

Later, when further searches were carried out, the men were warned to look out for a ploy the merchants were using to cheat the Customs. This was to obtain a licence to export poor quality wools known as 'Peltwoll, Cobwoll, Lambwoll and Malemort' and conceal good quality wool among these to avoid paying customs duties.

The sign of the Woolpack shows how wool was packaged for transport.

Inquisitions were also held at east coast ports to find out if wine was being correctly gauged. In several ports it had become the practice for merchants to bribe the King's gauger and his deputies, so that their tuns of wine, not containing the quantity required, were gauged and sealed with the gauger's seal as containing the correct amount.

Most of the smuggling on record at this time was through the ports by merchants, who either bribed officials or tried to conceal their goods. However, the King was also concerned about smuggling from the beaches and rivers and this concern was well-founded. One of the earliest known Norfolk owlers was William Warner of Knapton, a village near the north-east coast of the county. Warner was described as a common malefactor, who would help anyone to carry away the King's Custom overseas. In 1354 he was found guilty on three counts of selling wool on the seashore between Bromholm and Mundesley to foreigners who intended to take the wool abroad without paying customs duties. However, on the last occasion, after he had sold a cartload of wool to some foreigners, a storm prevented them from loading the wool aboard their ship. Warner then took the wool as far as a chapel at Paston where it was seized. He was fortunate because his plight was brought to the attention of Queen Isabella the King's mother, who was in residence at Castle Rising near Lynn, and at her request he was pardoned.

In order to make the collection of the wool tax more efficient, ten wool staple towns were created in England in 1353. Wool could only be sold in these towns; this had the administrative advantage that it centralised the collection, taxing and sale of wool for export. One town was Norwich, which was the main staple town in East Anglia. This seems to have had the effect of reducing smuggling in Norwich, and increasing it elsewhere in the county where regulations were more relaxed.

This was apparent in a report sent to the Exchequer in 1378 by the Collectors of the Custom at Great Yarmouth. They had arrested a ship named *La Godirad* of Fleading with uncustomed wool on board, which the master Simon Gybbeson and his partners had knowingly

Castle Rising. Queen Isabella was in residence here in 1354, when she secured a pardon for William Warner, an owler from Knapton.

allowed to be loaded. It was known that some of the woolfells belonged to one Simon Thurkyld of Great Yarmouth, but the names of those who owned the remainder were not known.

The report named several people who stole the King's Custom. It went on to say that there was a large number of foreigners either living in or visiting Yarmouth who bought and exported woolfells without paying customs duties, or sold them to others who exported them uncustomed. Local people were also involved in these practices and one Philip Skipstale, a Yarmouth weaver, was said to have sold wool and woolfells from his house to foreigners who loaded them aboard their ships at night to be exported without paying customs duties. The Crown ordered the Customers to sell the wools they had seized in Gybbeson's ship as 'dearly as possible and answer to the King for the proceeds'.

Although there were fewer reports of smuggling in Norwich, some uncustomed shipments did take place. In May 1391 John Broke, a merchant of the Hanse (Hanseatic League), was imprisoned in Norwich. He was charged with shipping wool to Flanders without paying customs duties. In his defence he claimed that his arrest and imprisonment was unlawful, as merchants of the Hanse and their goods were protected by charters granted by earlier monarchs against arrest. The King ordered the Constable of Norwich to release him and see that he was brought before the Chancery Court. Two other merchants stood surety for him for double the value of the wool.

Sheep grazing on the saltmarshes. For centuries wool was the mainstay of the owlers' trade.

During the fourteenth century the wool staple on the continent was moved from one town to another for reasons of politics, trade or defence. The staple was transferred between the towns of Antwerp, Bruges, Middelburg and St Omer, finally moving to Calais in 1392 where it remained until that town was lost to the French in 1558.

Moving the wool staple to Calais led to a great increase in

smuggling on the east coast. It was very difficult to smuggle wool through the Port of Calais as a close watch was kept on vessels arriving from England and their masters had to produce bills of discharge and clearance from their ports of departure. It was not surprising then that many of the merchants preferred to keep to the old established trading routes to the Dutch provinces when exporting their wool, thereby seriously undermining the lawful trade at Calais.

More evidence of large-scale smuggling through the east coast ports was supplied by William Stokes, an English merchant. In May 1411 he wrote to the Privy Council from the Dutch town of Middelburg in Zeeland informing them that in the five months since Christmas there had been many ships arriving in Holland, laden with large quantities of uncustomed merchandise. He said he did not know whether it was the fault of the customs officers, the clerks or the searchers. He reported that ships came from the Norfolk ports of Lynn and Great Yarmouth and in that short time 40,000 woolfells had been shipped from Lynn alone.

St Faith's village.
In 1411 John Meyer of St Faith's used the alias John Croft
for smuggling purposes.

Stokes went on to name two Norwich merchants, Robert Papingay and Martin Walsham, who had smuggled wool and 400 hides out of England in the ship of one William Pegge of Grimsby.

Among others mentioned were William van Burke of Yarmouth and John Meyer, alias John Croft of St Faith's, who continually conveyed wools out of the realm without paying customs duties.

Foreigners were heavily involved in east coast smuggling and Dutch smugglers regularly took their vessels into the smaller Norfolk harbours and coastal villages such as Brancaster, Cromer and Happisburgh where they could carry on their trade unhindered. Sometimes they would have the nerve to take their vessels into the main ports, as in 1415 when a Dutch boat from Zierikzee was discovered in Yarmouth with uncustomed wool, cloth and cheese on board. When the town bailiffs complained to the people of Zierikzee, they replied that the goods were the property of English merchants and that Hollanders would not get involved with smuggling.

Many priories in England were dependent on abbeys overseas. They often had large flocks of sheep and were thought to be involved in smuggling. This was shown in 1433 when the Crown set up a commission to look into the affairs of alien priories and two men were sent to check on these priories in Norfolk.

English merchants continued to ignore the Staple at Calais and smuggled their goods to the Dutch provinces. In the 1440s merchants sent a cargo of 50,000 woolfells in a ship from Lynn to Vere in Zeeland and the controller at Lynn seized 1200 woolfells which were then sold on behalf of the King for 2s.6d. each.

By the sixteenth century, merchants had adopted many ways of smuggling merchandise out of the country, and the goods smuggled were as diverse as fish and bell metal. A merchant sending a cargo by sea had to enter an obligation (bond) at the Custom House, naming the port at which the cargo was to be discharged. If the goods were unloaded at the port named in the bond, it was discharged by the customs officers or by the Exchequer. However, if the cargo was unloaded elsewhere the bond was forfeited.

In 1556, the *Elizabeth,* a Lowestoft vessel, sailed from Great Yarmouth with a cargo of herrings, which were to be discharged at Poole. The owner of the cargo was one George Wilson of Salisbury who handed John Thurston, the customs clerk at Yarmouth, a £200 bond to ensure the herrings were discharged at that port. It was later discovered that the herrings had been shipped to France. A Hemsby man, Gilbert Symkins, was examined before the Exchequer Court concerning this shipment. Symkins informed the court that he went to Yarmouth Custom House on Wilson's behalf where he was told that Wilson's bond had not been cancelled because the herrings had not been discharged at Poole. The bond had therefore been sent to the Exchequer. However, Thurston said that, for £8, he could help to get Wilson's bond discharged but could not do so for two or three terms. He advised that when the writs were issued at the end of each term, Wilson should pay the sheriff to send them back. By doing this for two or three terms Thurston would then be able to find friends to see the bond discharged.

A record of the outcome of this enquiry does not seem to have survived but it is clear from Symkins' evidence that to get his bond illegally cancelled Wilson would have had to pay the customer's clerk and the sheriff.

It was apparent that customs officers made use of their positions to make money for themselves and this was highlighted by the Merchant Strangers of London when they complained to the Privy Council in 1558. They claimed that customers and controllers of the Customs did not truly serve the Queen but used their offices to gain advantage and money for themselves. They asked the Queen to inquire into the way these men carried out their offices. They pointed out that by statute no customer, controller, or their deputies or clerks could own any part of shipping, wharves for loading or unloading, stock or merchandise. In spite of this, many of these men did in fact own great stocks and transported many of the wares and commodities prohibited by the statutes. The merchants also pointed out that when they went to the customer to make entries in his book of wares, his factors demanded to know about their goods before they were allowed to enter them in the book. If they did not sell the information to the factors, they were searched. Bribes and rewards were expected if merchants and others were to get their goods through the Customs. They went on to say that it was obvious to all men that when a poor man was appointed to the office of customer, or indeed his clerk, who kept the Custom House, he soon became rich. It was known that some men came into the office of customer's clerk 'without so much as a pair of hosen to their loins,' and within twelve years they were worth thousands of pounds.

In some ports it was an open secret that there was collusion between the customs officers and the merchants. King's Lynn was one such port. It was the natural port for Europe for much of

England, and its position on the banks of the Great Ouse, the outlet for several navigable rivers into the Wash, gave the port trade links with places well inland. These rivers flowed through several counties and were important trade routes along which goods were transported to and from the inland cities and towns. Since they flowed through some of the best agricultural land in England, it was not surprising that corn figured prominently in the commerce of the port. However, this trade was restricted by government controls and in the years of poor harvests the export of corn was forbidden, and at other times a licence was required.

The Tudor Corn Laws led to a great increase in smuggling and customs officials and merchants often worked together to their mutual advantage. Customs officials were not supposed to trade on their own account, but this did not stop Thomas Sydney, the Customer at King's Lynn, and Thomas Shaxton, a local merchant and alderman, from forming a business partnership. Sydney exported his corn in Shaxton's ships without a licence, and in 1572 he was called before the Exchequer to answer various charges but was only reprimanded. This was one of several reprimands he received, but he still managed to remain in office. This may have been due to the influence at court of his brother-in-law Sir Francis Walsingham.

Sydney's subordinates also found ways of lining their pockets at the expense of the Exchequer. Robert Daniel, the searcher, charged £3 a time to allow uncustomed cargoes to leave the port, while Richard Downes, a former junior clerk at Lynn Custom House, supplied blank customs receipts, cockets and clearances which he sold to the merchants at 13s. 4d. each. Downes had broken into the custom house and borrowed the seal of the port, had a cast made of it and returned it before it was missed. With this illegal seal and his experience in writing out these documents, he was able to produce convincing blank copies.

A similar situation prevailed in the port at Great Yarmouth. Much of the wine which was transported up the rivers Yare and Wensum to Norwich arrived without payment of customs duties. This was not surprising as William Smyth, the Customer at Yarmouth, illegally exported over 1,000 quarters of corn in 1569, an example which encouraged others employed at the custom house to get involved in smuggling. Henry Manship, a junior official at the Custom House, was caught smuggling wool abroad and loading ships with unlicensed corn at night. This did not prevent him eventually becoming controller at the port, and town clerk. He also became a freeman and was reputed to have written a history of the Borough.

When the Queen's army was abroad, some of the most lucrative contracts merchants could obtain were to supply provisions. Under cover of these contracts merchants, with the assistance of customs officials they had bribed, were able to smuggle large quantities of goods abroad. In the late sixteenth century, the merchants with these contracts employed a deputy, Henry Cox, to act for them. In September 1591, they instructed Cox to bribe Mr Owen, the Customer at Lynn, to allow their vessels to ship out of the port more wheat than shown on their licences. Cox was to offer Owen two hundred quarters of wheat licence or much more if he thought it was necessary to obtain his favour. It is not known whether Owen took up this offer.

The dishonesty of the officers was well known in many ports and some made no attempt to hide their activities. Little seems to have been done by the Crown to check the illegal practices which existed in the Customs Houses. By the early years of the seventeenth century fraud and corruption could be found at all levels of public service. Accepting bribes, or avoiding paying customs duties, was normal practice for many people. The attitude of the officers at the ports therefore had a considerable influence on the amount of merchandise smuggled out of the country, and the more corrupt the officers were, the more smuggling was likely to take place.

Smuggling was also of great concern to the East Anglian textile industry. In the 1620s it was known that some Norwich people were buying up various stuffs in large quantities for foreign merchants and, acting as brokers with the merchants' money, they exported the stuffs at the merchants' risk. They received a small allowance on every piece. The Privy Council warned the Mayor of Norwich and Norfolk Justices of the Peace that this practice was robbing the country of trade and commerce and defrauding His Majesty's Customs. The Council also warned that some Norwich people were daily buying up 'Kemmed Woolles' (combed wool), and worsted yarn, which they smuggled abroad to foreign merchants. They were ordered to investigate the dealings of those people and let the Council know what action they were taking before binding them over to appear before the Council to answer for their contempt.

A process used in the cloth trade to cleanse and thicken cloth was that of fulling, in which large quantities of fuller's earth was used, and to protect the trade, it was forbidden to export fuller's earth. However, a report made to His Majesty's Commissioners of Trade in 1625 stated that some earth suitable for fulling was being exported from Great Yarmouth. The report was sent to the Privy Council and the Yarmouth Customs officers were ordered to stop the export of fuller's earth and all other earth recently discovered in Norfolk suitable for the fulling process. The Yarmouth officers reacted by refusing to take any entries of earth for export. In spite of this, the Council was informed that some people had exported quantities of potter's earth, which was just as useful as fuller's earth in the fulling process.

After receiving this information it seems that the Privy Council felt the Yarmouth officers were not obeying its orders. The Council therefore requested that the Treasurer should order the officers at Yarmouth to stop all earth being exported from their area and account for the potter's earth already exported. It also demanded to know the names of the merchants and ship owners whose vessels had transported the earth so that it could order a fitting punishment.

Although exporting uncustomed wool was made a felony in 1661 merchants were still prepared to take the risk. In 1665, a Lynn merchant was found guilty of wool smuggling and fined £450, of which £250 was paid to an informer. Some merchants were prepared to defend their goods if officers tried to seize them. In 1664 two Norwich merchants, Peter Enton and George Symonds, were stopped by two Yarmouth officers while leading horses loaded with un-customed bags of silk. They immediately assaulted the officers and made good their escape. The Treasurer issued a warrant for their arrest.

By this time smuggling was so profitable that men other than merchants were involved. Mariners were often found guilty of smuggling cloth in and out of the country, or of making short entry in the customer's books. This was the case in 1661, when John Wigget, a mariner, petitioned the Treasury for the discharge of a parcel of Norwich stuffs that had been seized for short entry in the customer's books. His appeal was upheld and the Treasurer, the Earl of Southampton, ordered the Customs Commissioners to release Wigget's stuffs.

Wigget, however, was well known for his smuggling activities and, with one Thomas Prentice, was due to appear at the Norwich Summer Assizes in 1661, charged with smuggling linens into the country. This time the Treasurer was not so sympathetic and warned Sir Matthew Hale, who was to try them, that these men and their associates invented many ways of defrauding His Majesty's Revenue and worked together to weary the officers with 'vexatious suits and actions'. He recommended that the Justices paid attention to what the officers said and so encouraged them in the discharge of their duties. However, the Treasurer's appeal was in vain.

The Treasurer wanted the evidence given in court by customs officials to be unimpeachable. It was hardly surprising that little regard was given to this point of view when so many officers were themselves known to be guilty of smuggling and others were known to be in collusion with merchants.

Under the Commonwealth, a new excise tax was introduced by John Pym in 1643, and excise offices were opened throughout the country. This tax differed from customs duties in that it was the first buyer who had to pay it, so it affected everybody, including the poor. It was levied on ale, beer, cider, perry and strong waters, but was later extended to cover all imported beverages such as tea, coffee, sherbet and chocolate. Many new items were taxed, among them currants and tobacco. The tax was very unpopular and there were demonstrations against it in many parts of the country. In Norwich some tradesmen refused to pay the tax and the efforts of the magistrates, under pressure from the Government, to force them to do so resulted in violence and riots in which the brewers and butchers played a prominent part. However, the increase in the number of items taxed gave much more scope to the smugglers and led to a great increase in their trade and profits.

As time passed it became obvious that excise officers were just as liable to make use of their positions for personal gain as those in the customs. In September 1695, a man named Phillips detected several frauds committed by Samuel Dashwood, the Collector of the Excise for the County of Norfolk. He wrote to the Excise Commissioners informing them of his findings, which they passed on to the Treasury. As a result of the evidence supplied, Dashwood was found guilty and dismissed from his post.

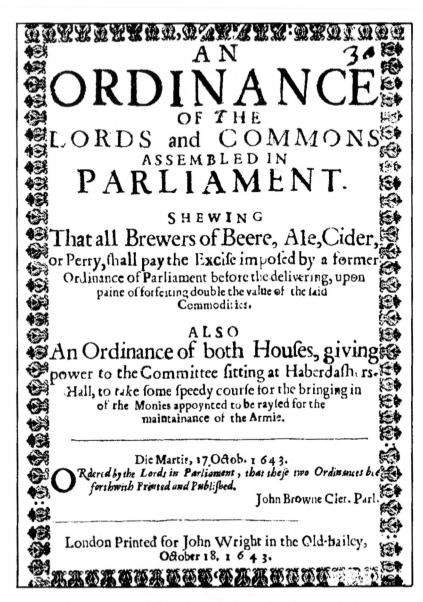

AN 3
ORDINANCE
OF THE
LORDS and COMMONS
ASSEMBLED IN
PARLIAMENT.

SHEWING

That all Brewers of Beere, Ale, Cider, or Perry, shall pay the Excise imposed by a former Ordinance of Parliament before the delivering, upon paine of forfeiting double the value of the said Commodities.

ALSO

An Ordinance of both Houses, giving power to the Committee sitting at Haberdashers-Hall, to take some speedy course for the bringing in of the Monies appoynted to be rayled for the maintainance of the Armie.

Die Martis, 17 Octob. 1643.

ORdered by the Lords in Parliament, that these two Ordinances be forthwith Printed and Published.

John Browne Cler. Parl.

London Printed for John Wright in the Old-bailey, October 18, 1643.

Two ordinances issued by the Long Parliament in 1643

By kind permission of H.M. Customs & Excise

It can be seen that export smuggling began in earnest when the first permanent customs system was introduced. As time passed, more items were taxed making it more profitable to smuggle goods out of the country. By the sixteenth century, it had long been a way of life for many people. Norwich, with its Dutch community, had many contacts in the Netherlands and it was therefore not surprising that the Strangers were able to recruit local people to buy stuffs for them.

In early times there is very little evidence of owlers operating from the beaches on the Norfolk coast. It may have been because the coastline was not adequately covered by customs officials, or because it was not difficult to get goods through the ports as officials could be so easily bribed. However, by the end of the seventeenth century, export smuggling had declined considerably and was rapidly taking second place to import smuggling.

King's Lynn Custom House, built in 1683.

2. Growth of Import Smuggling

During the reign of Charles II, 1660-1685, the Board of Customs was founded. One of the first changes the Board made at the ports was to introduce customs cutters to patrol the coasts. The Treasury gave the Customs Commissioners permission to build a boat at Yarmouth suitable for a master and a crew of four men. By the end of the century a fleet of fourteen customs cutters had been established. The Customs Commissioners also hired a small number of sloops and smacks at several ports, usually crewed by a master and six men. They were known as 'Custom House smacks' and were hired from private individuals principally to assist in preventing wool being smuggled out of the country. They seem to have met with little success as few convictions were recorded.

The position of master in one of these boats appears to have been much sought-after. When Daniel Darby, the master of the Yarmouth Custom House smack, died in 1714 he was replaced by one Bushy Mansell who was dismissed two years later. Peter Harold, the newly-appointed Surveyor at the Port of Norwich, left this office to take command of the smack.

It is clear that, at that time, some import smuggling was taking place in the country at large. An entry in the 1685 Excise Reports asked for a boarding boat to be provided to go alongside vessels and prevent brandy being run on the south coast.

In 1690 the jurisdiction of the two largest Norfolk ports, Great Yarmouth and King's Lynn, extended for several miles along the coast and for customs purposes all the smaller ports and harbours came under the control of one or other of these ports. The Customs in Norfolk were organised as follows:

Great Yarmouth Port

Name	Position	Annual salary
Thomas Clarke	Collector	£80
Edward Lawrence	Tide Surveyor	£50
Charles Lewis	Landwaiter	£30 + £10
Richard Bathurst		
John Jackson		

Richard West	Tidesman	£20
Richard Doughty		
Thomas Morse		
Henry Salthouse		
Robert Thompson		
Richard Mordyth		
Samuel Kirke	Weigher & Tidesman	£20 each
John Grahme	Boatman	£25
Daniell Derby		

Blakeney and Cley (Yarmouth Port)

John Wood	Collector, Waiter and Searcher	£20 + £20

Wells (Lynn Regis Port)

Owen Godfrey	Collector	£20 + £10
Roger Pedley	Waiter & Searcher	£15 + £10

Terrington Steep (Lynn Regis Port)

Edmund Edge	Boatman	£25

Heacham and Brancaster (Lynn Regis Port)

Richard Wight	Waiter & Searcher	£10 + £10

Lynn Regis Port

William Linstead	Collector	£70
Francis Challiner	Riding Surveyor from Wells to Lynn	£50 + £10
George Butler	Waiter	£25
William Gent		
Gabriell Cox	Boatman	
John Baily		
Robert Thetford	Tidesman	£15
John Townsend		
Edward Getting		
George Page		

The above shows that there were only three customs boats on the

Norfolk coast, at Great Yarmouth, King's Lynn and Terrington Steep. When necessary additional crew members were hired. They received no salary but had a share of the proceeds from the sale of any seizures they made. In general, the salaries were low, but the main source of their income was the fees that were paid by the merchants and importers on every transaction. There were so many scales of fees that the officers were often able to increase their salaries as much as tenfold. This system lasted until the early years of the nineteenth century when it was abolished.

During the last decade of the seventeenth century, there was a great increase in import duties of all kinds and various trade restrictions and prohibitions were introduced. This made it profitable to smuggle a variety of goods into the country and vast amounts of contraband were illegally brought in by English and foreign smugglers. Many boats were built just for the smuggling trade, and the introduction of 'fore and aft' rigging enabled vessels to tack and beat into the wind when close-hauled. Masters of these vessels could now sail into any creek, unload their goods and leave without worrying about the direction of the wind.

Since the Customs were originally organised to stop the owlers exporting wool and other commodities, how did the officers cope with this large influx of smuggled goods coming into the country?

In 1698 legislation was passed ordering the Lord High Admiral of England to direct naval vessels, from time to time, to patrol between North Foreland in Kent and the Isle of Wight, to assist in suppressing smuggling. Later, naval assistance was extended to other parts of the coast.

In the same year riding officers were appointed to patrol the south-east coast to check wool smuggling, but soon they were patrolling most of the English coastline. Their salaries varied from £25 to £60 per annum, out of which each had to support himself, a servant, and a horse. One of the earliest riding officers to be appointed to patrol the Norfolk coast was Richard Nash, the Riding Surveyor at Liverpool, who was appointed riding officer at Cromer in August 1703 with an annual salary of £50. Men applying for the posts of riding officers were usually recommended to the Customs Commissioners by local gentlemen of some standing, and these recommendations were passed to the Treasury. In 1717, several Norfolk gentlemen recommended one Thomas Faulk for some employment in the Customs. The Treasury Lords directed that Faulk should be presented 'to the first riding surveyor vacancy on the Norfolk coast, or some fit employment'. Later in October that year he replaced Robert Toll as a riding officer on that coast.

French goods were very popular in England and the constant demand for them ensured that large profits could be made by the French smugglers. In order to protect their interests on the English coasts the French smuggling vessels and their crews were well armed. It was not unusual for the French smugglers to run their goods by force of arms and thereby endanger the lives of the English customs officers who tried to interrupt their business transactions. It was a widespread practice of the French smugglers to exchange their goods for wool, which could easily be sold in France. There was also a strong Dutch influence on the east coast and large amounts of both wet and dry goods were brought across the North Sea from Holland by English and Dutch smugglers.

By the first decade of the eighteenth century, large quantities of smuggled goods were being run on the Norfolk coast and there was little the Great Yarmouth smack could do about it. This was shown in 1709 when Captain Darby attempted to board a Dutch vessel and seize 40 half-ankers (see Glossary) of brandy, which the Dutchman was trying to land. Darby and his men were attacked and badly beaten by the Dutch crew, and when he called out to a passing Gorleston vessel, his plea for assistance was ignored.

With so much contraband being landed on the Norfolk coast local people were well supplied with a variety of goods, both rich and poor being pleased to purchase the smuggler's wares. Perhaps the most important person in the county known to deal with smugglers was Sir Robert Walpole. Very little of the Dutch linen or brandy supplied to Houghton passed through the Norfolk Customs. Walpole's family was kept well supplied with goods and James Swanton, a smuggler from Wells, made regular calls at Houghton with Dutch linen. Even Walpole's old mother, who lived at Warham, loved to tell how she baffled the customs officers when she managed to get a load of contraband through her back door undetected.

Walpole also made use of his political contacts to smuggle wines into the country when he became a member of Prince George's Council in 1705. While serving on the Council he came into contact with Josiah Burchett, the Secretary to the Admiralty, and they became partners in a smuggling enterprise. This involved using the Admiralty launch to smuggle quantities of champagne and old burgundy up the Thames without paying duty at the Custom House. No doubt the bulk of those wines found their way to Walpole's house in Berkeley Street where he entertained his guests lavishly. Some years later when he held the office of Chancellor of the Exchequer he was still buying Dutch lace from the smugglers.

Walpole's dealings were not out of line with the political morality of his day. It was not unusual in his time for politicians to make use of the offices they held to promote their own financial advancement.

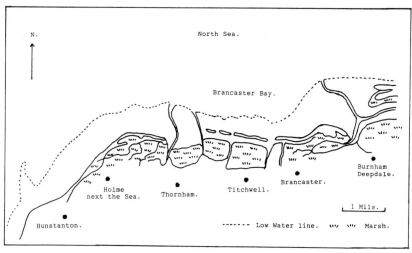

The North West Norfolk Coastline in the late Eighteenth Century
Some of the most notorious smuggling gangs operated in this area: their vessels anchored in Brancaster Bay to sell contraband to passing vessels.

The harbour at Brancaster was considered the best between Lynn and Yarmouth and the bay was generally the road where coasters or vessels, bound for overseas, anchored to wait for favourable tides. Without a boat stationed there it was impossible to inspect these vessels or others entering the many creeks on the extensive salt marshes. In 1710, after a visit to the Norfolk coast by the Surveyor General, recommendations from local officers and frequent reports that great quantities of goods were being run, the Customs Commissioners had a boat, crewed by two men, stationed at Brancaster. The boatmen, William Church and William Framingham, each received an annual salary of £25. It was reported that Church had been associated with the Customs at Cley for four years, and Framingham had been useful in discussions concerning customs frauds, in spite of being threatened by merchants.

In October 1718 William Lowndes, Secretary to the Treasury, sent a report to the Customs Commissioners containing a representation he had received from one Joseph King 'informing my Lords of the running of great quantities of goods on the coast of Norfolk'. Earlier that year Lowndes had reported a riot at King's Lynn in which customs officers had been beaten and abused, and some goods they had seized taken from them. The militia eventually restored order by capturing the smugglers and rioters. They were taken before the magistrates, convicted, and whipped round the town.

At this time the bulk of contraband coming into England did so virtually unhindered. Coasters sailing between Newcastle, Yarmouth and London often met French vessels hovering close to the shore ready to do business with their crews. Coasters not only unloaded their cargoes at the Norfolk ports of King's Lynn, Wells, Blakeney, Cley and Yarmouth but some, especially colliers, unloaded theirs on the beaches at Heacham, Hunstanton, Cromer and Mundesley. At Cromer, vessels up to 100 tons burthen could lie on the beach, where at ebb tides carts were drawn alongside to unload them. Contraband purchased from foreign vessels hovering off the coast could easily be concealed in these carts and carried inland.

In an attempt to stop vessels hovering off the coasts for smuggling purposes, Parliament passed the Hovering Act in 1718. The Act decreed that any vessel of 50 tons or less found within two leagues (about six miles) of the coast and beyond the limits specified on its licence without reasonable cause, could be seized. Later the laws were extended to cover vessels carrying more than four oars. These vessels could then be seized and cut into three parts. To combat this Act and subsequent Hovering Acts, it later became a favourite ploy of English and foreign smugglers, when they sailed from Dutch and French ports, to carry false papers, which stated that they were bound for x in Norway. Their intention, however, was either to run a cargo themselves, or sell it to coastal shipping on the English coast. If they were challenged by customs boats while hovering off the coast, they would produce their papers to prove they were bound for North Bergen and say that they were merely waiting for a suitable wind.

Not all English merchant ships were smugglers, but some recruited sailors who smuggled on their own account. They were not paid by the ships' owners, but worked their passage and had to make what they could by smuggling. If the ship was searched by Customs officers and their goods seized, they could end up getting nothing from their trip. Apparently the ships' owners were not held responsible for their crews' smuggling activities.

A decade or so later, the situation on the east coast had not changed and foreign smugglers were openly plying their trade. Evidence of this was shown in a report to the Customs Commissioners in 1729 from the Collectors and Comptrollers of the Customs at Great Yarmouth. According to the report, a great number of French vessels had been seen hovering off the east coast between Yarmouth and Newcastle. They lay close to the shore from where they sent their boats up the rivers, and publicly sold their brandy. The report went on to say that Captain Billop, whose cruiser had been sent by the Admiralty to assist the Customs officers, had been wounded and wanted the means to put a 'stop to such insults'. Appended to the report was a letter from Billop in which he described an encounter he had with French smugglers. He stated that on June 7th his cruiser sighted five French snows, small brig-like sailing boats. After a chase lasting one and a half hours, the smugglers suddenly laid to and engaged his cruiser. The action lasted two hours before the smugglers managed to get to the windward of his vessel and escape. Two of Billop's men were wounded and the cruiser's rigging was damaged. He pointed out that most French snows carried four guns and a crew of 25 to 30 men and that two of them were equal to his cruiser. Billop went on to say that several times he had chased four or five of them together off the coast, but this was the first time any had laid to and engaged him.

Captain Billop's concern about the situation on the east coast was well-founded, as the smugglers were virtually in control of parts of that coast. French brandy smugglers would not hesitate to attack English or Dutch smuggling vessels if they thought they were carrying brandy, the monopoly of which they wanted to keep for themselves. At the Lincolnshire port of Boston, the customs officers were intimidated by French vessels which manned their guns to avoid being disturbed while openly selling their brandy on the wharfs, where there was no shortage of customers. They threatened to take the customs sloop and her commander back to France with them if he tried to interfere with their trading.

Captain Harold, the commander of the Yarmouth cutter, was well known to French brandy smugglers who would have murdered him given the chance. This was shown in 1729 when the *Walpole* cutter, stationed at Wells, encountered two French vessels off the Norfolk coast, which were thought to have been supplying a fleet of colliers, anchored off the shore, with brandy. The *Walpole*, under the command of her mate, John Southgate, attempted to seize the French vessels. However, the French seized the *Walpole* instead and, mistaking Southgate for Captain Harold, would have murdered him had his correct identity not been made known to them.

Later, in 1736, the smugglers in the Boston area sent a letter to the Mayor threatening to set fire to the town if they were disturbed, and added that they did not fear the King's officers whatever their number.

The Custom House smacks were often no match for smuggling vessels which in many cases were much bigger, better armed, and carried more men. This situation was further aggravated by the war between England and France, 1741-48, when French privateers appeared on the east coast. A privateer was an armed vessel owned and officered by private individuals who held a commission, 'letters of marque', from a Government authorising them to capture merchant shipping of nations hostile to that Government. Privateers ranged in size from large ships with many guns to small rowing boats, specially fitted out to enable them to attack small defenceless traders or fishing boats. English and French privateers were constantly on the look-out for ships that they could seize and hold until a ransom was paid for their release. Many English and French smuggling vessels were also privateers and French smugglers usually brought contraband over to England and seized any English vessel they could to take back to France.

According to the Collector at Yarmouth his customs cutter was powerless against smuggling doggers armed with fourteen carriage guns and a naval sloop was necessary to combat these vessels.

The captains of the customs boats had to decide whether to challenge larger smuggling vessels, or to put the safety of their crews and boats first and allow the smugglers to go about their business unmolested. In January 1743 several ships on the Norfolk coast

31

witnessed an engagement off Mundesley between the Yarmouth Custom House smack and a smuggling vessel. Although smaller than the smuggler, the smack closed with her and fired three guns. The smuggler replied with nine guns and badly damaged the smack's rigging and sails thereby forcing her to retire. The smugglers were then audacious enough to hail the captain of the smack saying that they were all English and would like to drink a bowl of punch with him.

However, some of the smaller smuggling vessels or privateers could be taken quite easily by customs smacks. In November 1747, the Harwich smack sighted a small boat at anchor under Bawdsey cliff on the Suffolk coast. The smack approached the boat and hailed her, asking where she was from and where she was bound. Back came the reply in a foreign accent, 'Yarmouth to London.' The captain of the smack was suspicious and sent his boat with several armed men to board her. They met no resistance but found her to be a French privateer from Calais, equipped with small arms and carrying a crew of twelve men. She had come to the east coast hoping to capture some small defenceless trading vessels.

As far as smuggling was concerned, the revenue officers, even with the assistance of the Navy, could not stop or contain the enormous growth that took place in import smuggling during the first half of the eighteenth century. They had neither the manpower nor sufficient vessels capable of coping with the well-armed smuggling craft. The situation was further aggravated by the Government taxing commodities to finance the country's involvement in foreign wars; this led to a large increase in smuggling.

In the 1730s legal tea, on which 4s. per lb. duty had been paid, retailed in England for about 5s. per lb. However, tea from the East Indies could be purchased in Holland from 6d. per lb. according to quality. This made it possible for smugglers to purchase it and sell it in England for as little as 3s. per lb. and make a good profit. It also brought the price of tea within the reach of the labouring classes. Cheap, smuggled tea made it virtually impossible for the fair traders to sell their tea on which duty had been paid, and many of them became involved in smuggling tea themselves.

Since the early years of the eighteenth century, another spirit, 'geneva', had become very popular in England. Geneva (gin) was distilled from grain and flavoured with juniper berries. This Dutch spirit, sometimes referred to as Hollands, was said to have been introduced into the country by William III and English soldiers acquired a taste for it during the Dutch wars. It could be bought very cheaply and there was a big demand for it among the working classes of all ages. In London it was common for inns and shops to carry the sign, 'Drunk for 1d., Dead Drunk for 2d., Straw for nothing'. The straw was supplied so that the customer could sleep off the effects of the gin. There were 10,000 gin shops in London, and in 1728 it was alleged that gin-drinking was the reason for the death rate exceeding the birth rate. In order to check gin consumption, the Government imposed an excise licence of £20 on all retailers of spirits and placed a duty of 2s. on a gallon of gin. In 1736, the licence was increased to £50 and the duty to £1 per gallon. It was hoped that these increases would put the price of gin beyond the pockets of most of the population, but all it did was make gin a very attractive commodity to smuggle and force many retailers out of business.

Perhaps the attitude of many people in England towards smuggling was shown by a smuggler when he was sentenced to death in 1735. In his summing up, the judge had said that a smuggler was as great, if not greater, a criminal than a highwayman. However, the smuggler was not convinced by the judge's opinion and replied, 'A smuggler only steals, or rather conceals what is truly his own, as being fairly purchased by him for a valuable consideration, whereas the highwayman takes by violence what belongs to another.' He therefore thought that he should have been treated a little more leniently. He pointed out that high duties on goods destroyed industry, because no man could trade with a small stock where a great deal was paid to the state over and above the price of the commodity, and when a man could not live by trading in an open way, he would do so in a clandestine way.

Nevertheless the judge's opinion was shared by many people who feared that the smuggling gangs would soon threaten the civil authorities. It was also reported at this time in the *Gentleman's Magazine* that the smugglers in Norfolk and Suffolk went about in armed gangs of twenty to thirty men and frequently caused the customs officers to 'fly before them'. The *Norwich Mercury*, May 31st 1735, reported that a man on his way home to Morley had been pulled from his horse and robbed of about 10s., while a short distance away at Wattlefield near Wymondham the house of a man named

Shepherd was broken into and a considerable sum of money stolen. It was supposed that the robberies were committed by a gang of smugglers, 'who very much infest those places'.

How successful were the authorities in bringing smugglers to justice and detaining them while they were serving their sentences? The Government introduced the Smugglers' Act in 1736, in which the death penalty could be imposed on smugglers using arms. They could also face transportation, flogging or hard labour for resisting arrest. Harsh penalties could also be invoked against smugglers getting together in gangs.

Many of the smuggling gangs contained a strong criminal element. Hardened criminals were attracted to them and this was shown in March 1737 when three men were executed on Castle Hill in Norwich for a variety of crimes. The *Norwich Mercury* gave short accounts of the lives of two of them. One James Blade, alias John Johnson, alias Black Jack of the West, was about 41 years old. He was born at York, the son of a ship's carpenter. He did not want to learn his father's trade but wished to travel. After a while he joined a gang of smugglers, with whom he lived and spent a great deal of money. He then took up poaching and highway robbery. He robbed some people at Stanfield Green, near Mileham, and would have murdered them had his accomplice not stopped him. He also attended fairs in Norfolk, playing the unlawful games of 'picking at the girdle', or 'old hat', the 'thimble and balls' and the newly-devised game called 'the black joke, one of the greatest cheats ever invented'. He had nothing to say at the gallows when he died and his body was delivered to the surgeons to be anatomized.

Another was John Painter, aged about 35 years, who was born at Wimbotsham near Downham. His parents died when he was four years old and he was put out to nurse by the parish. When he was old enough he was given a warrener's job and eventually got married. After some years he rented a warren. Later he joined a gang of smugglers and worked for them as a servant. He was caught when he went to retrieve a parcel of tea he had hidden in a blacksmith's shop. When he was searched he had in his possession a firelock which appeared to be the breech end of a musket, cut off to about 9 inches long, loaded with a bullet and a quantity of small shot. He was also wanted for robbery and horse stealing. The report stated that at the gallows, 'he died as a very hardened creature'.

**A private in the
Norfolk Militia 1759.**

When it came to apprehending smugglers, regular soldiers were preferred to the militia, which could not always be trusted, and revenue officers usually sought the assistance of dragoons. The *Gentleman's Magazine* for 1738 published a speech made in the House of Lords in which the speaker claimed that the militia could not be trusted to assist in apprehending smugglers. 'This my Lords,' he said, 'is the case of smuggling on our sea coasts. I do not believe there are five out of twenty amongst our Militia who do not actually aid and abet the smugglers themselves, and would not be glad of every opportunity to favour them.'

Since the dragoons proved more reliable they were often called upon to arrest smugglers or to assist in their capture. A skirmish took place near the west Norfolk coast at Snettisham in July 1737. Four smugglers fought with a party of dragoons when they seized 7 cwt. of their tea. One of the smugglers' horses was killed and a soldier received a hand-wound before two of the smugglers were taken. They were committed to Norwich Castle and to foil any rescue attempts, they were escorted by 14 dragoons.

Without a strong escort, smugglers being transported between gaols stood a good chance of being rescued. In April 1751 when an outlawed smuggler named Fisher, of Diss, was arrested by customs officers they were immediately attacked by Robert Fisher, the smuggler's brother, and the prisoner escaped. Robert Fisher was eventually arrested and detained in the Castle for beating and wounding the officers.

In the eighteenth century rewards were being offered by the Government to people who supplied information which led to the capture and conviction of smugglers. Nevertheless people who informed against smugglers ran the risk of being attacked or even murdered. This was the case in 1745 at the Suffolk town of Beccles just over the south-east border of Norfolk. One night a man was pulled out of bed by smugglers who whipped him and tied him naked to a horse. They rode away with their prisoner who was never heard of again, although a £50 reward was offered. It was unlikely that anybody knowing what had happened to him, or who knew who the smugglers were, would have been tempted by the reward to give information to the authorities, for fear of meeting a similar fate.

Following legislation against smuggling in 1746, people convicted for running contraband were to face the death penalty, and those harbouring smugglers were to be outlawed and could be sentenced to death as felons. Known smugglers had their names printed in the *London Gazette* and were given forty days from the date of the publication to surrender themselves, or they would be adjudged guilty and have to face the death penalty. Whole communities could be punished if offenders were not convicted within six months. If seized goods were recaptured by the smugglers, the county could be fined £200. Any county in which a revenue officer was killed had to pay £100, or if an officer was wounded £40. A system of pardons and rewards was implemented for those who gave information which led to the conviction of two or more accomplices. These laws were intended to last for a trial period of seven years, but they remained on the Statute books until the 1820s.

With the introduction of these harsh new laws against smugglers and the system of pardons and rewards, the Government hoped to curb smuggling and get more assistance from the public in its fight against the smugglers than had previously been forthcoming. Was the Government's optimism justified and how successful were these laws in bringing smugglers to justice in Norfolk?

The forty days passed and none of the smugglers named in the *London Gazette* gave themselves up and they were therefore outlawed. Capture could now mean the death penalty for smugglers and not many of them were prepared to be arrested without putting up a fight. This was the situation when a wanted smuggler was taken on the outskirts of Norwich. The smuggler, Jeremiah Pratt, was described as over forty years old, five feet six inches tall, with a dark complexion pitted with smallpox. He was also known by at least twenty other names including John Wilson, Thomas Raynor, Mad Tom and Weasel. He was recognised and chased by several people until he was cornered at Lakenham. He managed to keep his pursuers at bay by threatening them with a brace of loaded pistols until two men arrived with guns and threatened to shoot him if he did not surrender. Apart from smuggling, he was wanted for horse stealing in Kent, Cambridge and Diss in Norfolk. He was also suspected of robbing the Yarmouth and Norwich coaches. He was tried, sentenced to death, and executed on Castle Hill in Norwich in April 1746.

The penalties for harbouring smugglers did not deter people from giving them refuge and several people were charged with that offence. In January 1748, Robert Osborn, a Norwich alehouse keeper, lost his licence and was committed to Norwich Castle for harbouring Robert Clark, alias Plunder, an outlawed smuggler. He was eventually escorted to London by a party of dragoons. The following year two other alehouse keepers were arrested and spent time in Norwich Castle. They were George Harrison of Palling on the Norfolk coast and John Sayer of Howe, seven miles south-east of Norwich. Henry Roads, a Hempnall man, was confined in the Castle on suspicion of harbouring Samuel Eager, alias Old York, an outlawed smuggler from Norwich. Roads died in the castle in October 1751 and Eager eventually died in Newgate Prison. This did not stop his widow handling contraband. She kept a small shop in St Martin's at Palace in Norwich, and twelve months after her husband's death a ¼ cwt. of tea was seized on her premises.

Several outlawed smugglers were arrested after the 1746 Act and their captors received rewards. Many of these arrests were made by a combination of revenue officers and dragoons. The following are some of the arrests made in the first five years after the Act and rewards paid.

Date	Arresting officers	Smugglers	Rewards
* Indicates an outlawed smuggler			
Jan. 1748	Mr Ramey, landwaiter, & dragoons	Samuel Wayman*	£500
March 1748	Mr Boyles, general surveyor of customs	Robert Cunningham* Tom Tit (an under-strapper)	£500

Dec. 1749	Customs officer and dragoons from Beccles	James Carbold* alias Jiffling Jack Charles Gowen* alias Papist of Beccles John Doe* Richard Parsons John Balderoy	£1500
June 1751	4 Dragoons from Diss	Thomas Brookes* alias Bricklayer Tom	£500?
1751	Dragoons from Norwich	Robert Young* alias Catchpole Galloway Tom* John Cunningham* William Cunningham* Another unnamed	£2500?

Most of the above smugglers were sent to London to be tried at the Old Bailey. It was necessary to provide a strong guard to prevent them escaping or being rescued while they were in transit. To avoid this happening, Samuel Wayman and later Robert Cunningham and Tom Tit were taken to the capital in the Yarmouth customs smack. James Carbold, Charles Gowen, John Doe, Richard Parsons and John Balderoy were sent to London in a coach and four, escorted by a strong guard of dragoons. It is also interesting to note that when Robert Young and his associates were arrested they were armed and disguised, both crimes under the Act. They were also wanted for housebreaking and murder in Suffolk.

There were several cases where officers made arrests well away from their own districts. Thomas Brookes was taken near Ely in Cambridgeshire by four dragoons from Diss in Norfolk. James Carbold and his associates were taken at Bramerton, near Norwich, by an officer and dragoons from the Suffolk town of Beccles. It would appear that one of the weaknesses of the reward system was that it tended to stop officers in different areas co-operating with each other when arresting smugglers. When officers in one area were informed of the whereabouts of smugglers in another area, even some miles away, they usually travelled to that area, made the arrests themselves and then claimed any reward. They did not inform the local officers, or they would have lost the reward, or had to share it with them. This also seems to have been the case when seizures of contraband were made. In August 1751, two Norwich excise officers found 300 lbs of tea in a cave at Buttlesly Green near Hoxne in Suffolk. The tea was sent to Norwich under the escort of a party of General Howard's dragoons.

There were so many smugglers operating in Norfolk to meet the large demand for contraband that customs and excise officers found making seizures from the well-armed gangs very difficult. Nevertheless the smugglers did not always have things their own way. In June 1733 a gang of 18 smugglers left the north Norfolk coast with 19 horses, each carrying nearly 2 cwt. of tea and other contraband. Thirteen officers pursued them from Cley and eventually caught up with them at Kimberley, near Wymondham. At first only one smuggler was prepared to put up a fight and while he and a customs officer were fighting one of his companions drew his pistol and fired at the officer. The shot missed and hit one of the smugglers in the chest, inflicting a serious wound from which he died a few days later. The officers seized the contraband and captured five of the smugglers, who were taken before a magistrate. He had them committed to Norwich Castle when they refused to find sureties.

Norwich Castle was the county gaol, and smugglers were detained there either to serve their sentences or to await their removal to London or elsewhere to stand trial. The castle was by no means escape-proof and prisoners, many of whom were smugglers, frequently escaped from confinement there. The ease with which some prisoners escaped is demonstrated by the five Kimberley smugglers who escaped on October 10th 1733, having been imprisoned there for nearly five months. At 7 o'clock in the morning they attacked the gaoler and took his keys, unlocked the doors and walked out. Their escape was well planned, as they were met by associates at the Castle footbridge who supplied them with pistols. With the pistols in their hands, they walked through the streets to the Brazen Doors, situated at the city wall entrance to All Saints Green, where five horses had been left for them by their comrades. As they rode off, they contemptuously threw the gaoler's keys on a nearby dunghill.

So many escape attempts were made from the castle that a guard of dragoons had to be mounted there to watch the prisoners in

August 1737, and in April four years later several breaches, made in the castle walls by smugglers, had to be repaired. Some prisoners escaped more than once. In November 1751, William Rose was one of the crew of a smuggling cutter, laden with Dutch gin and 5 cwt. of

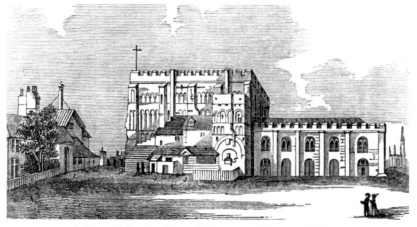

Norwich Castle and Sessions House, 1786.
Smugglers often escaped from confinement here in the
eighteenth century.

tea, taken in the act of running its cargo by the Yarmouth customs smack. He was sent under guard to Norwich Castle from where he made two successful escapes, only to be quickly recaptured.

One night in September 1753, Rose with Simon Fordham, James Clarke, two other smugglers and another prisoner, carried out an ingenious escape. They managed to acquire two poles, two strong ropes and several pieces of stick and, by removing their bedcords, were able to make a ladder. On the night of their escape they broke out of their cells. They tied the poles together to get maximum length, made a loop in one of the ropes, and with the aid of the poles managed to fix it to the top of the castle battlements. They climbed the rope to the battlements and then lowered themselves down to the roof of the Shirehouse, which in those days adjoined the Castle walls; from there they used the ladder to climb down and made off undetected.

Rose and Clarke were recaptured at Gorleston in the Queen's Head public house the following week, and were conducted under a strong guard to their old quarters in the castle. Fordham was also seen in the town, but made good his escape. However, two months later Rose and Clarke were two of the 16 prisoners, mainly smugglers, involved in another daring escape. At about 5 o'clock in the evening of December the 4th, the Governor's son and a gaoler went to lock up the prisoners for the night. They were suddenly seized by the prisoners who tied their necks and heels together and held them under guard. They waited beside the door until it was time for the other gaolers to return to let their colleagues out. Eventually one of the prisoners called, a gaoler opened the door and was promptly knocked senseless by two or three heavy blows. The prisoners made their escape, but four, including Rose and Clarke, were retaken in Norwich the same night having been unable to get their irons off. In the following weeks three other prisoners were retaken, two at Sileham in Suffolk and another at the port of Wells. Fisher, the Diss smuggler, managed to avoid capture by taking a ship to Holland.

William Rose finally left the castle in January 1757 after spending over five years there. As he was an excellent sailor, he was given a pardon on condition he served aboard one of His Majesty's warships for life. He was taken to Yarmouth and put aboard the first man-of-war to enter the port.

Smugglers planning to escape from the castle often needed equipment, which had to be smuggled in to them, and this made it necessary for them to have help from outside. Two such cases came to light in 1752 involving women. In June a woman, named Mary Andrews, smuggled saws and files to the prisoners. However, the gaolers became suspicious and carried out a search in which they discovered that several iron bars had been sawn through. Mary Andrews was arrested and the prisoners double-ironed, yoked and handcuffed. Later in August five prisoners did escape through a hole they had made in the Castle wall twelve feet above the ground. They used a rope to lower themselves. Ann Pain, who got her living by running errands for the prisoners, was arrested for supplying them with the rope. The two women were confined in the Castle to await their trials at the following assizes to be held at Thetford.

Some smugglers who escaped from the castle were especially difficult to recapture, as they often went abroad or spent much of their time at sea on smuggling vessels. It was when they landed between trips that they were vulnerable to arrest if their whereabouts became known to the authorities. One such smuggler was Robert

Shorten, who was sentenced to death at the Lent Assizes held on March 17th 1786, but later escaped from the Castle. He made several trips to Dunkirk in a smuggling cutter and after one trip he went to a public house in Flitcham, nine miles north-east of King's Lynn. It was there that he was recaptured in May 1787. Shorten strongly resisted his captors, but was eventually handcuffed. However, while they were in a blacksmith's shop he got his hands free, snatched up an iron bar and severely wounded one of the men who had arrested him with a blow on the back of the head, before making his escape. Shorten was soon recaptured and conveyed to the Castle. In December 1787 he was given a free pardon, but detained in the Castle on two Exchequer writs jointly amounting to nearly £2,000.

Smugglers were sometimes confined in the Castle for several years and some died there. In December 1777 it was reported in the *Norwich Mercury* that Godfrey Collings, a Yarmouth smuggler, had died in the Castle in his 77th year of age, having been imprisoned there for nearly four years. Ten years later the paper reported that William Southgate of Thornham, described as a notorious smuggler, commonly called Captain Southgate, had died in the Castle. He was being held on an Exchequer writ of £3,164.

The problems caused by the smuggling trade on the east coast were of course prevalent on the country's 6,000 miles of coastline. What was happening in Norfolk and off the coast reflected the situation nationally. Up to the end of the seventeenth century the Customs had been organised to combat the illegal export of wool, manufactured goods and other commodities. The Government had increased customs duties for a number of reasons, but chiefly to pay for the country's involvement in the War of the Spanish Succession and radically to reduce gin drinking at home. These increases made many commodities very profitable to smuggle, particularly gin. The Government, however, had not been prepared for the sudden growth in import smuggling and was slow to adjust to the changed circumstances.

Although the Government was repeatedly made aware of the serious threat to industry and the revenue from smuggling, little was done to improve the efficiency of the Customs and Excise services, or to increase the salaries of the officers. The Customs and Excise were two separate Government departments in the eighteenth century, but often co-operated with each other when searching for smuggled goods. The Customs had their warehouses in the ports and their vessels carried out patrols at sea, while their officers kept watch on land in the coastal areas and at some inland ports. The Excise had their officers in most of the larger towns throughout the country and were responsible for watching for smuggled goods from the coast and inland, although by the last quarter of the century they had several vessels of their own which enabled them to carry out sea patrols.

The effectiveness of many of the officers of the Customs and Excise was questionable when the age of serving officers and the quality of many of those recruited was taken into account. Since there was no official retirement age, men could work as long as they liked and many officers were old men. In July 1796 the *Norwich Mercury* reported the death of Thomas Griggs of Brancaster in his 92nd year. He was the oldest customs officer at the port of Wells. Later, in June 1807, the *Mercury* reported the death of Isaac Hoyle, the Surveyor of the Customs in Norwich. He was in his 78th year.

Some of the officers recruited were far from honest. In July 1776, George Kinch, a former excise officer in Norwich, who had been discharged for malpractices, was committed to the Castle charged with stealing a horse. He was charged on the oath of John Waits, an excise officer at Reepham, and was suspected of being an old offender who always managed to get off when tried. On his arrival at the Castle, he was searched and found to be carrying a loaded pistol. He then confessed to have pawned in the city four pistols, a silver watch, a brass key and other things. Later in March 1792 Thomas Sanderson, an Excise officer from Diss, was committed to the Castle charged with stealing a silver spoon from the King's Head Inn in that town.

It may have been the inadequate salaries of the Excise officers which were responsible for some of them abusing their trust. Thomas Paine of Thetford, the author of *The Rights of Man* and *The Age of Reason,* was a strong advocate for an increase in excise officers' salaries. In 1762 Paine became an excise officer, but was dismissed after three years for making false entries in his journal, showing that he had visited traders when he had not. In a letter to the Board, Paine apologised and asked to be reinstated. His apology was accepted and he eventually joined the Excise at Lewes in Sussex in 1768. He then wrote a pamphlet entitled *The Case of the Officers of Excise,* in which he outlined the reasons why excise officers should have their salaries increased. He pointed out that after paying his expenses, including the maintenance of a horse, an officer was left with only £32 per annum.

The pamphlet was signed by a committee of eight excise officers, including Paine, which claimed to represent all the excise officers in the country. More than four thousand copies were printed in 1772. They were sent to Members of Parliament, the Excise Commissioners and many influential people. It would appear that the pamphlet was supported in many areas. The *Norfolk Chronicle* reported in March 1772 that petitions were being sent from various parts of the country to the House of Commons, asking for the salaries of excise officers to be increased. The correspondent thought it was 'a precedent worthy of imitation, for when we consider the great advance [in price] of every necessary of life since the Excise was first established, and that mechanics and labourers of all kinds have nearly doubled their wages since that time the officers of the excise must have laboured under great difficulties'.

However, all the efforts of Thomas Paine and his supporters came to nothing because the Treasury refused to increase the salaries of excise officers. As for Paine, he was dismissed from the Excise in 1774 for being absent from his work without the Board's permission. At this time all the Norwich excise officers' salaries were paid out of money raised in St Gregory's Parish from the Land Tax, whether they were resident in that parish or not.

Although the lower ranks of the Customs and Excise were not well paid, some managed to accumulate large sums of money. In December 1785, the *Norwich Mercury* published an extract from a letter from Great Yarmouth. It concerned the death of Thomas Barber, a Custom House clerk. He had held this post for forty years and his salary was £80 per annum. He died after a short illness, and had only resigned his post a month earlier. When he died over £2,000 in specie was found in an old box in a closet in his bedroom, and a considerable number of crowns and half-crowns were discovered in the drawers of his bureau. The extract stated that his father had left him £700 and he had accumulated the rest from his salary. This however would seem unlikely, as he supported his widowed mother for many years and kept a servant up to the time of his death.

Not all the Customs and Excise officers were old or lawbreakers, and some of them showed courage when going about their duties, especially when outnumbered by smugglers. Although no smugglers were involved, the courage of a Norwich excise officer was shown in 1775, when the Norwich coach was held up at Ilford by five footpads. The officer, who was an outside passenger, fired a brace of pistols at the highwaymen, killing one of them. Seeing the guard unwilling to fire, the officer took his carbine from him and fired at one of the men, breaking both his legs. The wounded man was arrested but the others escaped.

With the suitability of many of the customs and excise officers in question, it was hardly surprising that the smuggling trade grew and flourished. At sea, when the first customs smacks were introduced, they needed the support of naval vessels. Even so they soon found that it was impossible to stop large quantities of goods being run into the country, as their craft were often outgunned by the well-armed smuggling vessels. On the land, the large well-organised gangs of smugglers posed a formidable problem for the customs and excise officers who often needed military assistance to combat them. The harsh laws passed by Parliament against smugglers did little to check the large numbers of people getting involved in the trade. It is clear from the number of smugglers held in Norwich Castle that the death penalty was not imposed on the majority of them. It may be that the smugglers who were executed were mainly those who were guilty of other crimes as well, such as murder or highway robbery.

3. Free Traders in Control

The high customs duties levied by the Government to pay for several wars ensured that smuggling would continue as a profitable occupation throughout the eighteenth century. These duties brought about an enormous increase in smuggling. Although spirits, and particularly geneva, were high on the list of smuggled goods at this time, it was tea that easily topped the list of dry goods illegally coming into the country. In 1759 the Government increased the duty on tea to help meet the cost of the country's involvement in the Seven Years War and this immediately made it a more attractive commodity to smuggle. Over the years the duties were gradually increased until by 1783 the tax on tea exceeded 120%, and by this time Britain had become a tea-drinking nation. It was estimated in 1765 that ninety families in every hundred drank tea twice a day. According to Arthur Young, farm labourers took time off from their work in the fields to brew their Bohea. The wealthy preferred to drink Congo, while the brews of the middle class were Singlo and Hyson.

Although a large proportion of the tea and geneva smuggled into Norfolk was for the London area, there was a good market for it locally, particularly in Norwich, and the larger county towns. The fact that the Customs and Excise were well represented at Great Yarmouth, one of the stations for their revenue vessels, did not deter smugglers from taking contraband into the town. In February 1768 Mr Joseph Ames, the mate of the customs smack, seized 37 half-ankers of brandy and geneva in a house near the North Gate, while on the same day the excise officers seized 20 half-ankers of geneva and 8 quarter-bags, containing 2 cwt. of tea, from a house near the Mendham Gates. Another seizure was reported in May 1775 when 400 half-ankers of geneva were taken from a vault near the North Gates.

Several other seizures reported in Yarmouth and the surrounding area in 1774 included a large quantity of tea on board a Dutch fishing boat in the harbour, and 150 half-ankers of gin and 14 bags of tea found in a hole near the gallows on Yarmouth Denes.

Norwich, with its larger population, offered a good market for contraband and many more seizures were reported in and around the city at this time. Indeed smugglers sometimes fought with excise officers in the streets to prevent their goods being seized. About nine o'clock one evening in March 1775, two excise officers stopped a mounted smuggler carrying a sack of tea near the Guildhall in the Market Place. A violent struggle took place and the smuggler received a cut across his hand before being pulled from his horse. Both the horse and the tea were confiscated.

Three years later, another incident took place in some gardens near the Cathedral Close when two excise officers confronted six men with a half-anker of geneva. The officers seized the geneva and were immediately attacked by the men. When one of the officers received a violent blow on his head from a stick, the other drew his hanger and severely wounded one of their assailants. The injured man had to be conveyed to the Norfolk and Norwich Hospital in a Hackney coach.

People who informed against smugglers put themselves and their property at risk. In 1780 Thomas Diggens was the innkeeper at West Raynham, four miles south-west of Fakenham. A gang of twenty smugglers had some of their goods seized which they valued at £60 and they suspected Diggens had informed against them and was responsible for their loss. One night the gang went to Diggens' house and broke in, smashing all the locks. Fortunately Diggens was away from home at the time, but they confined his wife and servants and damaged his property. The gang swore that they would murder him unless he paid them £60 for their goods. However Diggens' wife managed to escape and went to Lord Townshend at Raynham Hall. Lord Townshend and his servants immediately went to the assistance of the Diggens household, and when the smugglers heard of their approach they fled. It was some time before Diggens dared to return to his house and family, which was guarded by four dragoons. In March 1781, James Thompson, one of the smugglers, was arrested and committed to Norwich Castle for having, with others unknown, entered the dwelling-house of Thomas Diggens. He was held in custody until the Norfolk Assizes, which were held in August at Thetford, where he was found guilty and sentenced to death. He was later reprieved.

During the second half of the eighteenth century more goods were smuggled into Norfolk than ever before, and the many large well-armed gangs made it virtually impossible for revenue officers to make seizures without military assistance. This, however, was not

Lord Townshend, 1724–1807.
In 1780 he led his servants against a gang of smugglers who had
occupied the inn at West Raynham.

always forthcoming during the American War of Independence, 1775-1783, when most of the British army was serving overseas. At this time many of the duties normally carried out by regular soldiers were being performed by the militia. In some parts of the country, these men were not considered reliable when it came to seizing smuggled goods, as many were also involved in smuggling. During this war, the loss of command at sea by the British made life easier for sea smugglers bringing their goods from the Continent.

Without military escorts, captured smugglers were always liable to be rescued in transit. One Sunday morning in August 1775, several officers were conveying a smuggler from Yarmouth to Norwich Castle in a post-chaise when they were overtaken on the road between Acle and Burlingham by a number of well-armed smugglers. They threatened to shoot the driver if he did not stop and, when he did, they released the prisoner and rode off with him.

In the south-coast counties large gangs of smugglers were often seen carrying their goods across the countryside, many of them heading for London. This was also the case in Norfolk and Suffolk, and it was typical of what was happening regularly in these counties, when in October 1779 a gang of fifty well-armed smugglers picked up a cargo of contraband from the Norfolk coast near Cromer. The cargo, which consisted of tea, spirits, and other goods, thought to have been valued at some thousand pounds, was loaded on thirteen carriages and conveyed along the lanes and highways in a south-westerly direction for about 20 miles until the gang reached Shipdham. They stopped at a publican's in the village for refreshment, spending £28 before resuming their journey three hours later.

The advantage of goods being transported by large gangs was not only that there was less chance of them being seized, but that they could be conveyed directly from the coast to their destination without having to be taken secretly from one hiding place to another. Cargoes were collected in daylight, as these gangs were so well armed that revenue officers, or vessels, had almost no chance of stopping them. Sometimes revenue officers did not attempt to seize contraband from large gangs of smugglers, but merely watched at a distance in the hope of identifying some of them.

This may have been a wise course of action, considering what had happened some years earlier when the Yarmouth Excise Surveyor and five of his men were attacked by a gang of smugglers just south of

Yarmouth Haven. At midnight one night in February 1768, Mr Peter Haslip and his men were at sea when they intercepted a boat from a smuggling cutter, manned with seven men. It was laden with 160 half-ankers of liquor, and 700 lbs. of tea. After their boat had been seized, the smugglers asked to be taken ashore and Mr Haslip agreed. He sent two of his men to land them in the excise boat. When they reached the shore they were confronted by about 50 well-armed smugglers, some mounted and some on foot, who immediately seized the boat, secured the two excise men and demanded to know if they recognised anyone there. The excise men apparently did not, or had the good sense not to recognise any of them. Seventeen smugglers then put to sea in the excise boat, and savagely attacked Mr Haslip and his three men, beating them until 'some of their brains gushed out'. Mr Haslip and Jenkins, one of his boatmen, died from the wounds they received. The gang then ran the cargo unmolested, although one of them fell overboard and was lost at sea. The only smuggler to be arrested for these murders was Thomas Clevelong, alias Crab, who was tried at Thetford Assizes and found guilty of aiding and abetting the murder of Mr Haslip. He died at Newgate in December 1769.

Sometimes smugglers would try to intimidate revenue officers who were likely to get in their way when they went about their business. In August 1769 a gang of smugglers sent a letter to a customs officer stationed at Southwold on the Suffolk coast. The letter, which was written in red ink, stated that it was an emblem of a letter that would soon be written in his blood. Such a threat at this time would have added significance since it was only a few miles along the coast from where Mr Haslip and his boatman were murdered the previous year.

Who were the men involved in smuggling in Norfolk, particularly those in the large gangs? Most of the smuggling labourers working in Norfolk came from the county, but it was not unusual to find Norfolk men smuggling in Suffolk, or Suffolk men smuggling in Norfolk, or even mixed gangs of men from both counties. However, some of the gangs that travelled long distances consisted of men from the London area, or the southern counties, and it was not surprising that as several smuggling vessels from the Kent ports were seized on the Norfolk and Suffolk coasts, some of the gangs of smugglers came from that county.

In August 1780, a large gang of Kentish smugglers, consisting of 100 horses and men loaded with dry goods, passed by the Suffolk towns of Beccles and Bungay and through Harleston in Norfolk. Part of this gang came upon Mr Brock, an excise officer, in a public house in Yaxley, in Suffolk and, after a struggle in which he was badly beaten, he was dragged outside, tied across a horse and carried off. A party of light horse, in disguise, searched the countryside for him for miles around. However, the smugglers had put him aboard a cutter at Southwold, where he was detained until she was unloaded. When he was eventually released the captain of the cutter gave him a guinea, but he was unable to find his horse.

Easy money to be made from smuggling lured not only men who were otherwise employed in lawful occupations, but also law-breakers such as highwaymen, housebreakers and murderers. In November 1780, two armed highwaymen robbed several people on the turnpike road between Easton and Hockering. The men were part of a gang of smugglers, and when they were pursued they made off towards the coast. Another incident was recorded three years later, when two men stole a number of dollars from a ship in the Thames. They were eventually captured in Norfolk, having made their way to Thornham and then to Hunstanton in the hope of getting a passage to France or Holland on a smuggling cutter, but failing to do so.

Some of the most lawless gangs of smugglers on the east coast were to be found in the Hunstanton area, and men running from the law sometimes sought security by joining a gang of smugglers on that part of the coast. In April 1780, a naval press gang went into a public house in Boston in Lincolnshire to impress some bargemen. A struggle ensued, in which a sailor was seriously injured and one of the bargemen killed. The sailors were brought to trial and the jury found them guilty of wilful murder. Two of the sailors absconded and one of them was eventually arrested at Lynn, but it was reported that the other had escaped to a desperate gang of smugglers at Hunstanton.

Gangs in this area were just as well armed and prepared to fight to protect their goods as those anywhere else in the country. This was shown in July 1780, when the *Greyhound* customs cutter from Lynn came upon a smuggling vessel off Hunstanton. The cutter fired two guns at the smuggler which, having only three men on board, surrendered. Her cargo had already been landed and the rest of her crew were on the beach. The *Greyhound*'s crew immediately went to

Hunstanton Beach.
**In 1780 a skirmish took place here between the crew of the
Greyhound customs cutter and a gang of smugglers. One smuggler
was killed and several officers wounded.**

the shore in an attempt to seize the contraband, but were met with a warm reception from the smugglers. In the fight that followed one of the smugglers was shot dead and the *Greyhound*'s captain was shot through the thigh. With several of his men wounded, he was forced to retire into Lynn, taking with him the smuggling vessel.

An article on smuggling was written in the *Norwich Mercury*, November 18th 1780, claiming that smugglers were encouraged by the connivance of too many ill-disposed and self-interested people, and partly by defects in the laws. It was also reported that smuggling had reached such a height in the county that gangs of smugglers numbering from 30 to 50 men were often seen riding in the daytime in the 'most audacious and triumphant manner, from the coast through the middle of the county towards London, with carts and horses fully loaded, armed with firearms and other offensive weapons, to the great disturbance and terror of His Majesty's subjects'. The writer reminded the public of the gang which had recently broken into Mr Diggens' house at Raynham.

It was suggested in the article that the Government should

appoint a committee to inspect the laws against smuggling and to amend those that were deficient, or to make new laws by which such notorious offenders could be brought to justice. Other suggestions made were that the respectable gentlemen of the county should be putting such laws as had already been made into execution with 'firmness and intrepidity' thus becoming worthy magistrates zealous for the good of the community.

Finally the writer suggested that proper coasting vessels should be appointed to prevent the landing of smuggled goods. Some law was necessary to discourage the large numbers of 'stout, idle and disorderly persons from engaging in such dangerous traffic, the great nursery of highwaymen, housebreakers, and every desperate offender against the laws,' because of which no man's person or property was safe.

Public criticism of the magistrates and their lenient attitude towards smugglers had been mounting for some time throughout the country. Concern had also been expressed that smuggling attracted criminals of all kinds. Evidence of this was the petition sent to Parliament by the London and Westminster tea-dealers in March 1779. It pointed out the extraordinary extent to which smuggling was carried on by prisoners in the King's Bench and Fleet prisons. They had a continual supply of smuggled tea secretly conveyed to them, and not only did they keep open shops in the prisons, but employed men and women to duff and hawk for them in and about the metropolis. The petition also complained of the power given to the Commissioners of Customs and Excise and Justices of the Peace to reduce fines so that illicit dealers in tea, when detected, were being fined £5 instead of the full penalty of £100.

In 1780, the Government informed the public that every city, town and village throughout the country was involved in smuggling, much to the distress of the fair trader. It claimed that 3,870,000 gallons of geneva were being smuggled into England and Wales and up to 6,000,000 lbs. of tea illegally entered the country. The laws did little to check smuggling and in 1781, Lord Pembroke, commander of the 1st Regiment of Dragoons which had been billeted in Norwich during the winter of 1779-80, was moved to ask whether Washington would take America or the smugglers take England first - not an unreasonable question on the face of it. In the following years various estimates were given concerning the value of smuggled tea coming into the country and in 1783 the Board of Customs reported that tea smuggling had trebled and this illegal trade was worth about £7,000,000 per annum. However, in 1784, Pitt calculated that of the 13,000,000 lbs. consumed in the country yearly, 7,500,000 were imported without duty being paid.

In that year, Pitt almost wiped out tea smuggling by reducing the duty on tea from over 120% to 12½%. It was no longer a profitable commodity to smuggle and the sales of legal tea increased dramatically. It is possible to get some idea of the effect this reduction of duties had on smuggling in Norfolk by listing the number of tea seizures reported in the *Norwich Mercury* and the *Norfolk Chronicle*, for the ten years either side of 1784. In the preceding years, 48 tea seizures were reported, many of which were of considerable quantities, while in the following years 6 seizures were reported, only one of which was a large amount. After 1794, no tea seizures appear to have been reported for 23 years. In contrast, by studying the tobacco seizures in the same way, there were only two seizures of tobacco reported before 1784, but in the following years 26 were reported. It would appear from these figures that many of the tea smugglers turned to tobacco smuggling after 1784, to recoup their losses. Those to benefit the most were the honest tea dealers, who at last got the reduction in tea duties they had been campaigning for.

By reducing tea duties, Pitt had effectively curbed smuggling in this commodity, but smuggling in other articles, particularly spirits, was as high as ever and the laws were being openly flouted. The situation in Norfolk was shown when a correspondent wrote in the *Norwich Mercury*, September 17th 1785, that he wished to bring to the attention of the magistrates a public nuisance that was too prevalent in the county, and particularly in the Hundreds of North and South Erpingham. He referred to the number of small private houses in most of the villages in that area where spiritous liquors were sold in open defiance of the laws. He went on to say that they were not only 'a refuge for idle and dissipated wretches who assemble on the Sabbath day but were constant harbours of poachers and smugglers'. He continued, saying that he hoped the parish officers would take steps to crush these 'seminaries of vice'. The writer took the precaution of remaining anonymous, signing himself 'A well-wisher of the community'.

The towns and villages in these Hundreds include Sheringham,

Cromer and Mundesley on the coast, and Aylsham, Buxton, Cawston and Coltishall inland. However, as the writer indicated, this was happening throughout the county and showed how ineffective were the laws against smuggling.

Pitt's Act of 1784 may have curbed tea smuggling but it did not put an end to the large gangs of smugglers operating throughout the country. In Norfolk the smugglers would have had little trouble recruiting labourers to assist them in transporting their goods, as unemployment was high at this time, particularly in Norwich. In October 1785, a large body of men paraded in the city streets begging for money. The magistrates said that, although they sympathised with the distress of the poor and would help them legally to seek relief, all such unwarrantable associations must stop. They ordered the constables to arrest anyone they found begging in the streets.

However, the customs and excise officers did not always lose out to the smugglers and for two or three years the excise officers at Wells met with some success against them in the Hunstanton area. Mr Bliss, the Supervisor, and two officers, William Spencer and Thomas Abbot, often assisted by dragoons, made several seizures of contraband. In February 1780, with military assistance, they seized 1,000 gallons of foreign geneva, about 400 lbs. of tea and 260 lbs. of camphire (?camphor or camphene), from a gang of smugglers at Hunstanton. The following November, Bliss and Abbot, with a party of Lord Townshend's dragoons, seized, at some unspecified location, 500 gallons of foreign brandy and 9 bags of tea.

The successful run of seizures made by these officers came to an end on December 31st 1782 when, in company with a dragoon, they were attacked at Thornham by a gang of smugglers armed with firearms, pokers and pitchforks, and some 26 lb. bags of tea they had seized were rescued. Mr Bliss received six serious head wounds, which crippled him, and the smugglers threatened to murder the officers.

The officers recognised only one of their assailants, Thomas Franklin, a well-known smuggler, and a warrant was issued at King's Lynn for his arrest. A naval press gang was enlisted to assist the peace officers in apprehending him. Franklin was soon arrested, but when his associates heard he was taken, they pursued the peace officers and sailors and after a short scuffle they rescued him. Franklin returned home to find a wedding reception being held at his house. Shortly after this a party of West Norfolk Militia arrived, surrounded the house, and called on him to surrender. In the confusion that followed, the command to fire was heard by the Militia, from whom nobody knew, and a volley was fired into the house. This resulted in the death of a tailor named Nichols, who was shot through the heart. Two women were also wounded; one was shot in her arm and the other received an ear wound. Franklin, seeing that it was impossible to escape, surrendered and was taken before a magistrate who committed him to Norwich Castle whither he was escorted by a strong guard of the West Norfolk Battalion. No further reports concerning Mr Bliss were recorded and it would appear that his injuries forced him to retire.

When the American War of Independence was over, more soldiers became available to assist the revenue officers. It was reported that one Monday in October 1783, two wagons loaded with gin and tea had been taken from smugglers near Happisburgh and conveyed to Yarmouth Custom House. The report continued, stating that the following evening a party of light horse was sent from Norwich to Happisburgh to assist the Custom House officers because the smugglers were so numerous in that area.

Even with the assistance of soldiers, it was very difficult to seize contraband without meeting resistance from the smugglers. Within a few days of Franklin's capture, a large seizure was made by some officers and dragoons at Hunstanton. The smugglers quickly assembled and were assisted by many others armed with pokers, clubs and other weapons. They attacked the officers and soldiers and managed to rescue some bags of tea. However, the captain of the smuggling cutter involved in the incident received serious cuts in his shoulders and several others were badly injured before the skirmish was concluded.

Incidents between customs and excise officers and smugglers regularly took place at this time and some people seem to have attacked them simply because they were revenue officers. In the same week as the above skirmish, Mr Jewel, an officer of the Customs at Cley, was on the road travelling from Blakeney to Morston, when a man on horseback rode up to him. The rider suddenly produced a bludgeon from under his coat and struck the officer a heavy blow on his head, which was badly cut. It was with great difficulty that Mr Jewel managed to reach Morston.

At this time some people were calling for magistrates to carry out the laws against smuggling, but how effective were the courts when smugglers appeared before them? Two incidents took place in September 1784 that led to smugglers appearing before the Assize Court. The first occurred on Hunstanton beach, when some excise officers and soldiers seized a quantity of contraband goods that had been landed from a cutter hovering off the coast. The seizure was made by Green and Bennett, two excise officers, with a party of General Elliot's light horse, and the goods were temporarily lodged in a house in Hunstanton.

William Kemble, or Campbell as it is written in some reports, the captain of the smuggling cutter, planned to rescue the goods and armed himself and his crew for that purpose. However, he was warned that the officers had been reinforced by another party of light horse, and were about to set out again in the hope of seizing another cargo. Kemble decided to change his plan; instead of attacking the house, he planned to ambush the officers and their escort in a narrow lane through which he knew they would have to pass. Armed with carbines and bayonets the smugglers concealed themselves behind a hedge to await the revenue party. When the unsuspecting party arrived, Kemble and his men fired a volley through the hedge instantly killing William Webb, a young dragoon, who was shot four times in his chest. Mr Green was shot through his body, the ball entering one side and coming out of the other, leaving a wound from which he died the following day. Another officer was seriously wounded in his thigh and a horse was shot from under one of the soldiers.

In spite of their surprise, the remainder of the party attacked the smugglers and captured Kemble and two of his men, Henry Gunton and Thomas Williams, while the other smugglers escaped. The prisoners were taken before a magistrate who committed them to Norwich Castle. Several weapons taken from the smugglers had the Tower stamp on them and may have been taken from soldiers disarmed by the smugglers in earlier encounters.

Thomas Williams turned King's evidence and Kemble and Gunton appeared before the Norfolk Assizes in March 1785, charged with the murders of the dragoon and the officer. These men were obviously guilty and were expected to be found so by the Court; however, much to everyone's surprise, the jury found them 'not guilty'. Mr Murphy, counsel for the prosecution, stated that if a Norfolk jury was determined not to convict persons guilty of the most atrocious crimes, simply because they were smugglers and had the sympathy of the people, there was an end to all justice. He then moved for a new trial, ordering a fresh indictment and that none of the jury should be permitted to sit at the second trial. Consequently, they were tried again on the evidence and the new jury was out of court for three hours before returning to bring in a verdict of 'not guilty'. Kemble and Gunton were released and carried on smuggling

until a warship captured Kemble's boat off Wells in 1786, and took it into Hull. It is possible that Kemble was taken into Hull instead of one of the Norfolk ports because he would not be known there and would not get the sympathy of the public as he had in Norfolk. Whatever the reason for taking him into Hull, it would seem that his smuggling activities came to an end as there appears to be no further record of him.

The graves of Mr Green and William Webb can be seen in Hunstanton churchyard and the inscription on the latter's tombstone reads:-

'In Memory of William Webb, late of the 15th Lt. D'ns,
who was shot from his horse by a party of smugglers
on the 26 Sep 1784.
Aged 26 Years.
I am not dead but sleepeth here,
And when the Trumpet Sound I will appear.
Four balls thro' me Pearced there way:
Hard it was. I'd no time to pray
This stone that you Do see
My Comerades erected for the sake of me'.

The inscription on Mr Green's tombstone reads as follows:-

'Here Lie
The mangled remains
of poor William Green
an Honest Officer of
Government Who
in the Faithful
discharge of his
duty was inhumanly
murdered by a gang of
smugglers in this Sept
27th 1784.
Aged 37'.

The verdicts of Coroners' inquests also showed partiality towards the smugglers. On June 12th 1777, John Pitcher was one of a smuggling gang at Cley when their goods were seized by Luke Vernon, the Deputy Comptroller of the Customs at Cley, assisted by dragoons from the Queen's Regiment. A scuffle took place and Vernon ordered one of the smugglers' horses to be shot. A pistol was fired at the horse and Pitcher was unfortunately wounded in his knee. Four months later Pitcher died and, at a Coroner's inquest, Luke Vernon was accused of wilful murder. In August 1778, the officer appeared before the Assize Court and was acquitted, as no case could be found against him. Several 'respectable gentlemen' gave him good character references but more important was the evidence of the doctor who attended Pitcher. He maintained that Pitcher did not die from his wound, but from dropsy, induced 'by a very intemperate use of spiritous liquors'.

Another Coroner's inquest was held in August 1784, when Mr Jay, the second mate of the *Hunter* Customs cutter stationed at Great Yarmouth, was murdered by Charles Gee, a Bacton smuggler, in front of at least twelve witnesses. The verdict of the inquest was 'Wilful murder by persons unknown'. (See p. 77)

With the smugglers literally getting away with murder in the courts it is not surprising that they were prepared to attack revenue officers and their assistants. In November 1784, Mr Lockwood, an excise officer at Caister, seized some contraband from some smugglers on the causeway. The smugglers left the scene, but one returned later to rescue the goods and beat Mr Lockwood in a 'cruel manner'. The smuggler was later arrested and taken before the Mayor of Great Yarmouth who committed him to gaol.

A typical encounter took place one night in February 1794 when Mr Bridden, a Norwich excise officer, was on his way to Shotesham. It was about midnight when he came upon two horses, pulling a cart loaded with spirits and tobacco. When he tried to seize the cart, the two smugglers accompanying it pelted him with stones until he was forced to retreat empty-handed.

The revenue officers, of course, did have some success against the smugglers. In May 1782 several officers travelled from Edinburgh to arrest a smuggler in Norfolk. The smuggler had been confined in Edinburgh Castle ten years earlier for a crime described as heinous in nature. He escaped from the castle and eventually found his way to Burnham Deepdale on the north Norfolk coast. A reward of several hundred pounds was offered for his recapture. He took up smuggling and was successful for a number of years until his vessel was seized off the Norfolk coast. As a result of this seizure, his whereabouts became known to his former captors in Edinburgh. A strong party of men left Edinburgh in post chaises and when they arrived at Burnham Deepdale they trapped the smuggler in his house. They had to break open several doors before they could arrest him and he was immediately taken to King's Lynn.

It is clear that the large smuggling gangs went about their business with little regard for the law. Contraband was landed on the Norfolk coast and openly transported to various destinations, some as distant as London. The revenue officers had little chance of seizing contraband without the assistance of soldiers. The well-armed smugglers were prepared to inflict serious injury or even to kill those who opposed them. This was hardly surprising when public sympathy was so much with the smugglers that they literally got away with murder. Fear that the smugglers would soon take over the country was expressed in Parliament. It is therefore reasonable to say that the free traders were in control at this time.

4. Norwich and the Fair Traders

Throughout the eighteenth century, the Norfolk fair traders had cause to complain about the smuggling trade. Norwich, one of the largest provincial cities, was a good market for smuggled goods and large quantities of contraband were purchased there. However, not all the inhabitants of the city looked favourably upon the activities of the smugglers. In 1720 one Charles Cock took to the Treasury a petition, signed by twenty-five Norwich dealers in brandy, tea and coffee, complaining that smuggling had reduced fair trading in the area and was responsible for a decline in their business. They stated that French brandy was sold locally at the same price at which they paid duty, and that people were frequently supplied with the very best tea, green and Bohea, at 6s. and 7s. per lb. Coffee and chocolate were also sold at a 'proportionate under rate'. Finally, they proposed to pay the wages of a riding officer and recommended the bearer of the petition for the job. Soon after this initiative by the Norwich traders, twenty London distillers sent a petition to the Treasury supporting the Norwich petition, and complaining that they also were 'threatened by the same evil practice'.

In Norwich the customs and excise were constantly on the alert for contraband being smuggled into the city. When their suspicions were aroused, the officers would search people, horse-drawn vehicles, packhorses and buildings if they thought they were concealing contraband. 'Duffers' were people who tried to conceal smuggled goods on their person; their bulky appearance often attracted the attention of the officers. In January 1731 a Yarmouth woman tried to take a considerable quantity of tea and silk handkerchiefs into the city hidden in her clothes. When she was stopped and searched by customs officers they discovered several pounds of tea quilted into her petticoat.

Three seizures were made by two Norwich excise officers in December 1733. They took 4 cwt. of tea from a house in St Augustine's parish, 100 lbs. of tea from 'a poor woman's house' at Trowse and another 100 lbs. were also seized locally. Commenting on these seizures the *Norwich Mercury* stated that by this practice the fair traders may know what is meant by the popular cry 'No Excise'.

While carrying out their night patrols the city watchmen sometimes interrupted smugglers delivering their goods. One night, in June 1739, the Watch in East Wymer Ward came upon two armed horsemen standing some distance apart. As they approached, the men rode away. At that moment, a man carrying a sack on his shoulder came along. One of the watch stopped him and enquired about the contents of the sack, whereupon the man threw the sack down and ran away. When the sack was opened it was found to contain half a cwt. of tea. Later the same morning, two other sacks of tea were found in a yard, which were thought to have been thrown over a wall. A search was made of a neighbouring house and a large number of tea-filled cannisters were discovered. Altogether 2 cwt. of tea was seized.

In October 1752 it was reported that a watchman had stopped a man carrying a sack near the Red Well in the city. He took the sack from the man and discovered it contained two oilskin bags of tea, which he seized. Soon afterwards two horsemen rode up and tried to snatch the sack, but the watchman held on to it and his loud cries forced them to retreat. Two hours later 26 lbs. of tea was taken from the house of Mrs Eager, the widow of a Norwich smuggler who died in Newgate prison.

French brandy was a profitable commodity to smuggle into England, where it retailed at 7s. or 8s. a gallon, duty paid. The following advertisement appeared in the *Norwich Mercury*, August 24th-31st, 1728.

'Just Now Imported
A large quantity of the best French Brandy, which will be sold neat and unadulterated, at 7/- per Gallon, with a permit. Also an extraordinary Vinous Brandy, at 5/- per gallon: and a very pleasant Tobacco at 12d per lb. Sold at the Black Boy and Still in Dove Lane Norwich.
By Will(iam) Furly'.

In France a smuggler could purchase a tub of just over 4 gallons, nearly a half-anker, of the best brandy for 16s. and sell it in England at a profit.

Some Norfolk traders, however, smuggled goods on their own account, or dealt with the smugglers. This went on for many years and it was reported in June 1751 that four Norfolk people had been fined for dealing in smuggled tea and one, an old offender, was fined £110. Some years later, in March 1764, three Norwich dealers in spiritous liquors were prosecuted for fraudulently receiving Dutch gin into their stock 'to the manifest injury of the Revenue and discouragement of the fair dealers'. They appeared before the Mayor, Thomas Churchman, and had to pay heavy fines.

Tubs roped in this way could be slung over the smuggler's shoulders or over the back of a pony.

It was not surprising that with so much contraband coming into the county the fair traders found their profits greatly reduced. The *Norwich Mercury,* June 6th 1778, reported that a meeting had been held at the White Hart in the city by the principal tea dealers, at which it was unanimously agreed to present a petition to Parliament. The petition was to ask for a bill to be passed which would effectively prevent the smuggling of tea and spirits into the country, 'an evil so injurious both to the Revenue and the honest trader'. It was thought that similar petitions would be sent by all the capital trading towns in the country.

By the end of January the following year, petitions had already been sent to Parliament by the counties of Norfolk, Suffolk, Essex and Kent, the corporations of Maidstone, Yarmouth and Bristol and most other counties, cities and boroughs. At this time the Norwich petition had been passed through the city parishes and signed by the Mayor, Sheriffs, Justices, Aldermen, merchants, manufacturers, freemen and freeholders. To discourage smuggling the petition asked for the inland duty to be taken off tea, which it was hoped would also remove the greater evil of adulterating it. The petition also asked for an Act to amend the Act passed in the previous session of Parliament, which ruled that 6 lbs. of dried leaves were not seizable, but 7 lbs. and over were. It was pointed out that if the 6 lbs. of leaves were frequently replaced great damage could be done to the trade.

A copy of the Norwich petition was sent to the town of Rye in Sussex, where large quantities of goods were being smuggled. The following letter sent from that town to the Mayor of Norwich shows how the petition influenced people there.

'To the Right Worshipful
Mayor of Norwich.

Sir,

I received the copy of the Petition to be presented to Parliament by the worthy Members of Norwich, in order to prevent smuggling, & etc so very injurious to every honest Tradesman -

I requested a meeting of the principal tradesmen, and waited on Thomas Philip Lamb, Esq; Mayor; who desired the whole corporation to assemble at the Town Hall at 11 o'clock today, who all agreed upon petitioning in like manner - Mr Mayor wrote a very genteel letter to the Hon. Thomas Onslow and William Dickinson, Esq; the Representatives in Parliament for this Town, desiring their good endeavours to suppress smuggling, promote the honest trade of this Kingdom and to consult with the Representatives of Norwich, Maidstone, and other petitioning counties.

Sir, Your most humble Servant
R. Pellard.

Rye, Jan. 12 1779.'

In the same month, the *Norwich Mercury* reported that smuggling had reached a height unprecedented in this or any other nation in Europe, and that a speaker in the House of Lords had stated that the Revenue was being defrauded of £3,170,233 per annum, which was a moderate calculation as tobacco, snuff, French wines and many other articles were not included in that sum. He further stated that smuggling had become a matter of serious consideration, as also was the dangerous practice of adulterating tea.

At this time, adulterated tea was causing great concern in many parts of the country. The demand for tea was so great that it could not be met by the smugglers in the normal way. This led to tea being adulterated by unscrupulous dealers and others. These people adulterated tea by re-using tea-leaves that had already been brewed, or the leaves of ash, elder, sloe, liquorice and other trees, shrubs and plants with Terra Japonica, logwood and copperas. The finished product was then sold to the smugglers who passed it on to their customers, thereby creating a serious health risk as tea was consumed in such large quantities throughout the land. In fact, the adulteration of tea was considered a far worse crime than smuggling. It was reported in the *London Evening Post*, November 26th 1778, that Phillips, Lloyd and Co., large tea dealers in Grace Church Street, London, were tried and convicted of manufacturing certain leaves in imitation of tea and selling great quantities to the smugglers.

How much adulterated tea was sold in Norfolk is a difficult question to answer, but there is evidence that Norwich people were concerned about it when it was mentioned in the Norwich petition to Parliament. In another incident at that time, two men offered coffee for sale in the city. After they had left Norwich, the Excise Office was informed and three officers, Weeks, Gedge and Dunmow, pursued them and caught up with them at a public house on the edge of Poringland Heath. They searched the men but could find nothing in their possession, except a bag containing about 3 or 4 stone of tasteless powder which resembled Scotch Snuff; they therefore allowed the men to go on their way. The following week the Norwich Excise Office received samples of powders seized on the premises of three London tea dealers convicted of making imitation tea. When Henry Weeks saw the samples, one of which resembled Scotch Snuff, he said it was the same as the powder in the bag belonging to the men they had searched at Poringland. Another sample was like 'rappee', a coarse kind of snuff, and another was perfectly black, which was thought to be some ingredient used to stain or dye the leaves of imitation tea.

However, gangs of smugglers were still taking large quantities of contraband into Norwich. In January 1779, it was reported that early one Saturday morning fifty smugglers and horses loaded with tea had been seen passing the Cringleford tollgate. As they approached the city they dispersed: thirty-three entered Norwich through St Giles' Gate and three of them made their way to Duke's Palace Yard, where they were stopped by excise officers. One horse and its load were seized but the smugglers managed to escape.

St Giles's Gate, Norwich.
In January 1779, thirty-three smugglers, with packhorses loaded
with tea, entered the city through this gate.

The *Norwich Mercury,* June 19th 1779, reported that there had
been several seizures made within a few days in Norwich, and that
scarcely a night went by without large gangs of smugglers passing
through the city. Two days earlier a gang of smugglers, with about
twenty horses loaded with tea, passed through St Stephen's Gate at
2 o'clock in the morning. However they were seen by the Militia, who
were on guard, and chased along the road to Chapel Field. Three
smugglers dismounted and ran off leaving their horses with some

'dollops' (see Glossary) of tea to be seized by the soldiers. The following week the gatekeeper at St Stephen's was dismissed by the Court of Mayoralty for letting this gang of smugglers into the city.

St Stephen's Gate, Norwich.
In 1779 the gatekeeper was dismissed for allowing
smugglers into the city.

Although most of the contraband at this time seems to have entered the city through the twelve gates, some smugglers made use of the River Wensum. One evening, in the same month, smugglers tried to get a quantity of gin into the city by the river. They went up the river in a boat loaded with several half-ankers and quietly tied up at St Ann's Staithe in Conesford Ward. Just as they were about to land the tubs, some officers hidden nearby jumped into the boat and seized the cargo.

Not all the contraband coming into Norwich was for local consumption. One day in 1783 the York stage wagon left the city with 1½ cwt. of tea and some spirits hidden aboard. Information was received at the Excise Office in Tombland concerning these items and an officer with a party of dragoons left the city in pursuit. They overtook the wagon near Thetford and seized the contraband.

As shown in the petition, many Norwich people, and especially the honest traders, wanted the Government to pass laws which would put an end to smuggling. However, some people were prepared to take action themselves against men they thought were smugglers. In July 1779 the Lynn coach arrived at the White Swan in the Haymarket. On board were a naval lieutenant and his press gang. They had been subpoenaed to stand trial for impressing the servants of an important Lynn merchant. A rumour soon spread in the city that they were smugglers armed with pistols. Several people then got together and arrested them. They were detained for several hours before the lieutenant arrived with the subpoenas and they were released.

Another incident took place one night in March the following year, when a Mr Punchard, a Norwich man, was returning home from Scottow Fair. He was stopped by three dragoons who accused him of being a smuggler, which he denied. A struggle took place and Mr Punchard was left with a badly bruised head. The assault was reported and the dragoons were arrested and taken before the Mayor. They were ordered to make satisfaction to Mr Punchard, which they did, and were released.

By this time the Government had passed an Act in which dealers and traders could bring prosecutions against people who were involved in smuggling. In London the distillers, grocers, tea-dealers and other traders, whose businesses had been affected by the illegal trade, formed themselves into an association and accepted subscriptions, the proceeds from which were to be used to prosecute people involved in smuggling.

A similar Association 'for the carrying into execution the Act of Parliament against smuggling' was formed in Norwich in July 1779, and a subscription was opened in the city, which it was thought would be well supported. The Act directed that by August 1st all dealers in tea, coffee, chocolate, coconuts etc. had to have the words 'Dealers in Tea, Coffee, Chocolate, Coconuts, etc.' painted on some conspicuous part of their premises. Failure to comply with this would mean a fine of £200, while importers of spirits and publicans who failed to display the words 'Dealer in Foreign Spiritous Liquors' on their premises would be fined £50. One half of these fines were to go to the King, and the other to the prosecutor. People who had the correct words over their premises would be recognised as legal dealers, and anyone buying articles from dealers whose premises were not so distinguished or from duffers, or hawkers, who secretly sold these articles at markets, fairs, or from house to house, would be fined £10 for every offence. The sellers could also inform against the buyers and receive a share of any fine imposed and be fully acquitted of their own offences. Offenders who could not pay their fines could be sent to prison until their fines were paid.

The next meeting of the Association was arranged for Monday August 2nd, at Johnson's Coffee House in the city, and the public were instructed that all informations given, and letters sent, were to go to the secretary of the Association or the Mayor's officers.

When the Association met on August 2nd, it was pointed out that any dealer buying an article, for example tea, from a person who did not have the words 'Dealer in Tea' over his premises would be fined £100. Justices of the Peace could summon any person, other than the accused, to give evidence and if they refused to appear or give evidence they would be fined £10. It was noted that two people were already being prosecuted for this. The public were warned that those buying or selling tea, coffee, rum, brandy or geneva, illegally, had a good chance of being convicted as nobody knew which member of a family or neighbourhood would be summoned to give evidence. It was also stated that a summons directed at any person by their correct or assumed name, and left at the house, warehouse, cellar, or that person's usual place of residence, was deemed legal.

It was further stated that £1,000 had already been subscribed in the city and it was thought that the subscription would become large and general, not just in Norwich, but throughout the whole county of Norfolk. It was pointed out that the Government had made 'proper laws against the great national evil of smuggling', and it was for people to see that these laws were carried out. Dealers were also warned that if they made false entries in their excise books they would be fined £100. The meeting was then adjourned.

In spite of these warnings, some people continued to buy goods from illegal premises, hawkers and strangers. Buying from strangers proved a costly practice for a man when he bought two bags of tea at the Duke's Palace public house in Norwich, in June 1787. Two men who were lodging there offered the bags for sale claiming that they contained 60 lbs. of tea. After inspecting a sample the man purchased the bags for £8. Later when he opened them he was shocked to discover that they only contained about 4 lbs. of tea, the rest being made up of sand and sawdust. The bags had been so cunningly packed that a cut made in any part of them would reveal only tea. However, by this time the strangers had already moved on after robbing their lodgings.

It would seem that the Norwich Association had little or no impact on smuggling in Norwich; the early enthusiasm of its members and subscribers appears to have waned quickly. However, at first, the new laws may have worried the smugglers' 'more respectable' customers. It was now an offence to purchase contraband at the door and the smuggler could inform against his customers, for which he would receive half of any fine imposed and be acquitted of his own offences. The laws were aimed at discouraging the customers and therefore it was necessary for a high degree of trust and co-operation to exist between the smugglers and their customers. Since many criminals were involved in smuggling it was necessary for the customer to be very careful to deal with smugglers he could trust. One customer, a regular visitor to Norwich at this time, was Parson Woodforde of Weston Longville. The entry in his diary for May 17th 1780 tells that he had stayed up until 12 o'clock at night because he expected 'Richard Andrews the honest smuggler' to bring him some gin. It would seem that Woodforde had to prove to himself that he was not dealing with criminals but smugglers, who otherwise followed lawful occupations, and whom he knew he could trust.

Government reductions in tea duties, first in 1750 and again in 1784 when Pitt reduced the duty to 12½%, did improve matters, but smuggling was rife in many other commodities. In the early years of the nineteenth century, concern was expressed about the number of gin shops in Norwich. At the Norwich Quarter Sessions, held in January 1813, Mr Steward Alderson called attention to 'a species of nuisance existing in various parts of the town, which not only endangered the public peace but also the public health and morals. If the magistrates had signed licences of such houses, it was wholly through ignorance of the sort of houses to which they were giving their sanctions'.

During the eighteenth century, it was clear that the smugglers could easily undersell the fair traders, making it very difficult for them to continue in business. Some therefore resorted to dealing with the smugglers while others sought the aid of Parliament. The petitions sent to Parliament and the associations formed to finance prosecutions against smugglers had little effect and, although the tea dealers benefited by the large reduction in tea duty, the other fair traders had little to show for their efforts.

Seizures reported in and around Norwich

Date	Contraband	Where seizure was made
1752	Tea, 16 lb.	Mr William Lombe's house, St Andrew's parish
1764	Geneva, several bottles	Bread cart from Wells, near the city
1772	Geneva, several half-ankers	Stables at the back of the Theatre Royal
1773	Geneva, several half-ankers, and tea	Fish dealers in Cockey Lane
1774	Geneva, 15 half-ankers	Pig sty at Mile Cross
1774	Tea and geneva	Cart and two horses near St Stephen's Gate
1775	Tea, 5 cwt.	Lime Kiln House, Harford Bridge
1776	Spirits, several half-ankers	Two carrier carts at Magdalen Gate
1776	Geneva, 27 half-ankers	Barn at Eaton
1782	Gin, 24 half-ankers	A garden near the Brazen Doors
1785	Lace and other dry goods valued at £2,000	On Tombland
1787	Tea, large quantity	Cat & Fiddle Public House
1790	Gin	Cart in Magdalen Street
1791	Tea, 2 cwt.	Yard in Golden Ball Lane
1791	Tea and spirits	A house in St Peter's
1791	Geneva, 20 half-ankers	Cart near St Augustine's Gate
1791	Spirits, 18 half-ankers Tobacco, 50 lbs.	On Magdalen Fairstead
1792	Geneva 16 galls. Tea, 65 lbs. Tobacco, 240 lbs. Snuff 50 lbs.	Road between Spixworth and Catton

5. The Conflict at Sea

It is clear that smuggling developed into an enormous industry during the eighteenth century and that towards the end of that century the fair traders in Norfolk and elsewhere were desperate for new laws to curb it. The massive growth in import smuggling led to changes in the Revenue services and it became necessary to recruit more men. The first line of defence against the smugglers was at sea, and in an attempt to suppress smuggling both revenue and naval vessels were employed.

When the duty on tea was reduced in 1750, smuggling became less profitable and the trade in contraband declined. However the situation gradually changed when the Seven Years War broke out in 1756, and the duties on goods were increased. This made the illegal trade very profitable and, over the years, smuggling grew to such an extent that by the end of the century more contraband was coming into the country than ever before. It is not surprising then that this period was referred to as the 'heyday of smuggling'.

During this time there was a big increase in smuggling by the passengers crossing from the continent on packet boats, and contraband was often seized when coaches bound for London from the ports were stopped and searched by excise officers. For some time smuggling had been carried on by passengers on packet boats at Dover and Harwich. Sons of the gentry returning from the Grand Tour were no exception when it came to smuggling goods they had purchased abroad. In 1741 William Windham of Felbrigg Hall in Norfolk was staying in Geneva while on the Grand Tour. When Robert Price, one of his friends, returned to England in October, he wrote to Windham describing how he smuggled some landscape paintings by Bursiri through the Customs at Dover in his fiddle case.

The demand for contraband grew to such an extent that new industries were created in foreign ports to supply the English smuggling trade. In 1749, one Thomas Bevan escaped from England to the French port of Boulogne, where he established a woollen manufacturing industry. At this time many outlawed smugglers and others arrived at the port and formed themselves into a company 'to promote the practice of smuggling'. Others set up a business to manufacture hats, and ships arrived daily with supplies of coney wool (rabbit skins). Tea was usually smuggled in oilskin bags and industries to manufacture these were set up in the Dutch ports of Rotterdam and Flushing and the French port of Dunkirk.

A coaster in Yarmouth Roads.
The crews of these vessels often bought goods from smugglers at sea.

Selling contraband to coastal vessels and fishing boats at sea had been going on for many years. Therefore it was no surprise in April 1763 when a fleet of 30 colliers arrived at Harwich and reported that they had encountered 10 smuggling cutters, which offered them contraband goods. It was known that these cutters regularly cruised off the Norfolk, Suffolk and Essex coasts, paying little regard to the revenue cutters on these coasts. One of these vessels, the *Good Intent* of Rochester, had been chased several times by revenue cutters before she was eventually seized in 1768. Her crew had boarded several vessels offering to sell contraband liquor, and when she was taken, Thomas Williams of Happisburgh was searched and £46 in gold and silver was discovered concealed between his thighs in a leather bag and a worsted purse.

Buying and selling contraband at sea caused problems for two brigs from the Norfolk port of Wells in 1765. They were both seized at sea and one, the *Constant Friends,* had 30 gallons of spirits and 40 lbs of tea on board. Her master maintained that he did not know they were on board and that they had been taken aboard from the 60-ton *Norfolk* at sea. The *Norfolk* was searched by customs officers and 28 gallons of spirits and 10 lbs. of tea were found on board. She was allowed to resume her voyage to Woodbridge in Suffolk, with two officers on board. Mr Hall, her owner, sacked the master and offered to pay £106 to redeem her. The fate of the *Constant Friends* does not appear to have been recorded.

Another smuggling vessel working the east coast was the *George* of Hull. In 1769 she sailed from Hamburg for King's Lynn. On her arrival in the Wash, her crew buried 150 half-ankers of spirits in the sands at Lynn Deeps. She then entered the harbour and took on a cargo of timber, after which she put to sea. On her outward voyage her crew recovered the tubs at Lynn Deeps and hid them under the timber. As she continued on her passage to Harwich, she disposed of 106 tubs, but the Customs had been informed and on her arrival at her destination she was searched by Cyprian Bridge, and 42 tubs were found on board. The *George* was promptly seized, condemned and later burnt. Cyprian Bridge, the Commander of the Harwich revenue cutter, received a reward at the rate of 10s. a ton.

A similar fate was met by a smuggling cutter when she was seized carrying a large cargo of spirits. The *James and Polly* landed 80 tubs at Cromer and 150 half-ankers elsewhere on the Norfolk coast, which were picked up by a gang of mounted smugglers. She was bound for Sizewell Gap, on the Suffolk coast, to deliver the rest of her cargo when she encountered the *Argus* customs cutter from Harwich. The smuggling vessel was immediately seized when the customs officers boarded her and discovered her cargo of contraband liquor. She was burned at the same time as the *George.*

The Netherlands had long been an important outlet for goods smuggled by English export smugglers, particularly from the east coast of England. It was not surprising therefore that when import smuggling increased and became very profitable, Holland became one of the main suppliers of geneva and tea. The principal foreign port from which goods were smuggled into the east coast of England was the Dutch port of Flushing. A correspondent who had been staying in

Flushing for twelve weeks sent an account of what he had seen there to the *Norwich Mercury* in January 1779. He said that there were 30 cutters employed in smuggling goods 'on our coast'. All had letters of marque; they carried from 10 three-pounder guns to 20 six-pounder guns and had crews numbering from 30 to 60 men. These vessels carried cargoes varying from 10 to 50 tons of tea and 500 to 2,000 half-ankers of geneva each voyage. He also stated that the small unarmed smuggling boats went regularly into the French ports. In a report published the following month, the *Mercury* described the port as 'the home of the English smuggling outlaws'. In a Government pamphlet entitled *Advice to the Unwary* published later that year, it was claimed that the Dutch town of Schiedam distilled 3,867,500 gallons of geneva annually, the bulk of which was for smuggling into England through Flushing. The pamphlet also claimed that a distillery had been set up for making geneva at Dunkirk and that the French imported 5,000,000 or 6,000,000 lbs of tea, most of which was for smuggling into England.

It was a common complaint by customs officers that their cutters were no match for the large smuggling vessels and this was the case for much of the eighteenth century. In 1778 a list was compiled by the Harwich customs officers of eight of the large smuggling vessels which frequented the Essex, Suffolk and Norfolk coasts. It was thought unlikely that the *Argus* and the *Bee* revenue cutters stationed at that port would be able to take any of them. The most formidable vessel on the list was 134 tons burthen, armed with 12 guns and manned by a crew of 45 men.

However, one of the vessels on the list was taken two years later by the revenue cutter stationed at Boston in Lincolnshire. Commanded by a man called Baker, she appears to have been a Norfolk vessel of 112 tons burthen, carrying 10 guns and a crew of 28 men. She was taken on the coast near Brancaster, carrying a large cargo, mainly tea and spirits. Her crew consisted of Norfolk men and they were all taken and secured.

The larger smuggling vessels could, and did, sail close to the coast and unload their cargoes on the beaches, in daylight, with no fear of interruption from revenue officers or vessels. This was the case one Monday afternoon in August 1780. At about 4 o'clock, a smuggling vessel mounting 14 carriage guns appeared off Cromer and landed £2,000 worth of dry goods. A gang of 50 smugglers who had been waiting on the shore carried the goods inland. A Custom House smack lay nearby observing the proceedings, but her crew were outnumbered and she was too lightly armed to risk a fight with the smugglers. At best the customs officers aboard the smack could only observe the proceedings and hope to identify individual smugglers for future reference.

Sometimes these large smuggling vessels would encounter His Majesty's warships at sea, and if they had a large cargo of contraband, they were well worth taking. In June 1780 two warships, the *Ariadne* and the *Fly* sloop, arrived in Yarmouth harbour with two smuggling cutters from Flushing, which were laden with 6 tons of tea and 1200 casks of liquor. One of the cutters was the 150-ton *Deception* of Folkestone, armed with 16 carriage guns, consisting of 3- and 4-pounders and a crew of 29 men. The other was the 70-ton *Three Brothers* of Sandgate, carrying a crew of 9 men and armed with four swivel guns and small arms.

How successful then were the revenue cutters in seizing smuggling vessels at this time? Without assistance from the Royal Navy the revenue cutters and smacks could only realistically challenge the smaller smuggling craft. However, Captain Fisher, the resourceful skipper of the Yarmouth Custom House smack, used his wits to capture a large English lugger in April 1779. This lugger had letters of marque and was armed with six mounted carriage guns and several swivel guns. She arrived one night off Lowestoft and sent her large boat, manned by fifteen of her crew, ashore with a valuable cargo of tea. The following day the smack sighted her off Pakefield and Captain Fisher, knowing his smack would be outgunned if he approached her, decided to try to outwit the smugglers. A large fleet of colliers was anchored there so he circulated a report among them that the lugger was a French privateer. The sea was calm and the scene was peaceful, when suddenly the entire fleet of colliers opened fire on her. The smuggler, still short of fifteen men and subjected to continuous fire from the colliers, struck her colours and was seized by Captain Fisher and a large number of men from the colliers. The lugger was taken into Yarmouth where she was found to be carrying 600 casks of geneva and brandy and over 300 bags of tea.

The crews of some smuggling vessels violently resisted any attempt by revenue officers to board their craft and were even prepared to commit murder. On August 10th 1784, when the Great

Yarmouth customs cutter, the *Hunter,* under Captain Fisher, encountered a smuggling lugger off Beckhythe, near Overstrand, Fisher could not get close to her because his vessel was becalmed. He manned his ten-oared boat with twelve men under the command of his second mate, Mr Jay, and they rowed towards the smuggler. On approaching the vessel they recognised it as a Bacton lugger, whose master was Charles Gee. They made several attempts to board her, but were beaten off by the crew. She was carrying four large cohorns (see Glossary) and a good supply of small arms. The smugglers fired several shots into the customs boat and, in order to destroy her crew, they unshipped one of their cohorns and hurled it into the boat. Fortunately it lodged upon an oarsman's bench and did little damage, but the smugglers kept up their assault, throwing an axe, a pistol they could not fire and a large powder horn at the men in the rowing boat below. In spite of this, Mr Jay made a determined attempt to board the lugger, but Gee fired a blunderbuss at him, killing him instantly. Finding the mate dead, the crew pulled for the shore and, in spite of their pleas, Gee and his men continued to fire at them until they reached the beach at Bacton where they carried the body ashore.

The following day an inquest was held and notwithstanding the positive evidence given against Gee, the jury returned the verdict 'Wilful murder by persons unknown'. The same evening the body was interred at Bacton. It was covered by the *Hunter*'s ensign and carried by the twelve eyewitnesses to the murder. It would appear that Charles Gee was never tried for the murder of Mr Jay and presumably carried on smuggling.

At this time English coastal waters were not safe for merchant shipping. Apart from smuggling vessels and English, French and American privateers, pirates were also active. The large profits to be gained from smuggling encouraged privateers and pirates to become involved in the trade. In fact a midshipman, Fall, aboard the naval sloop, *Alderney,* deserted and became captain of a French smuggling privateer and was regarded as a pirate in England. Fall spent much of his time smuggling and hovering off the east coast where he regularly attacked shipping. In 1780 the naval cutter, *Liberty,* commanded by Captain Berkley, arrived off the coast and carried out an unsuccessful search for him. It was reported in the *Norwich Mercury* that between February and April 1782 Fall had captured eighteen vessels on the east coast, all of which had been ransomed.

Reports of vessels captured off the Norfolk coast were common. In March 1782 when a boat arrived at Lynn with a cargo of groceries, the captain reported that he had witnessed a sloop captured off Cromer by a black American privateer carrying fourteen carriage guns. At this time loyalty to one's own country seems to have mattered little to some men, when profits were to be made. This was shown in January 1782, when a smuggling vessel landed a cargo of tea, brandy, sugar and tobacco near Aldeburgh on the Suffolk coast. The crew of the vessel were mostly Englishmen, several from Suffolk, but she was commissioned by both the French and Americans as a privateer. Having discharged her cargo, she put to sea and encountered an English coastal vessel, which she promptly seized and carried off to France for ransom purposes.

It was not just shipping that lived in fear of smuggling pirates and privateers, but also the coastal towns and villages. In February 1781, eleven men armed with muskets and cutlasses landed at Runton on the north Norfolk coast from a lug sail boat flying the Dutch colours. However, they were arrested and committed to Norwich Castle. They insisted that they were smugglers and part of a 30-man crew of a sloop that had left Flushing a month earlier. It would appear that they preferred to face a charge of smuggling, where they were likely to get more sympathy, instead of piracy, which carried the death penalty. They were eventually taken under a strong guard to the Nore.

Although people were prepared to see smugglers escape from the law, at this time, pirates were severely dealt with. In 1781 William Pain, a pirate, was hanged in London and his body was taken to Great Yarmouth where it was gibbetted on the North Denes.

Two years later, a smuggling cutter from Hunstanton, commanded by Benjamin Royal, anchored off the village of Trimingham. Her crew went ashore and plundered several houses of beds, and all the butter and cheese they could lay their hands on, threatening to murder all those who resisted them and set fire to their houses. Having secured its provisions, the cutter sailed for Flushing. A report of this robbery was immediately sent to Yarmouth in the hope that a naval cutter would be able to intercept Royal's vessel before it got clear of the coast. However, there was no report of any capture being made.

This situation continued during the Napoleonic wars and the inhabitants of Blakeney on the north Norfolk coast were greatly

**Trimingham, which was plundered of bedding and victuals in 1783
by smugglers who wanted provisions for their vessel.**

alarmed in February 1795 when they received information that a
smuggling lugger from Flushing lay in the harbour with twelve six-
pounder guns and a chest of small arms hidden in its hold. The crew,
consisting of at least eighteen men, were under orders to make
reprisals on corn vessels both in and off the harbour. One evening,
about nine o'clock, the principal merchants assembled armed with
pistols and cutlasses. Led by Mr Buck, the local excise officer, they
took the King's boat and went alongside the lugger and boarded her.
They searched the vessel but found nothing incriminating, the lugger
having landed her cargo some days earlier. However, some of the
crew behaved in an 'awkward and prevaricating manner' and were
therefore looked upon with suspicion by her captors. They were
escorted into the village where they were interrogated for about four
hours, before being released the next morning, as they had committed
no offence. After reporting the above incident the *Norwich Mercury*
warned people living near small harbours how important it was in
those critical times to keep a close watch on every lugger or cutter,
and search them when there was the slightest doubt about their
intentions.

When the war with France began in 1793 many revenue vessels, including the Great Yarmouth cutters, the *Hunter* of the Customs and the *Lively* of the Excise, took up letters of marque. This entitled them to seize any vessel on the high seas and receive prize money for doing so. The risks were small as few merchantmen were heavily armed or capable of putting up much resistance. On the other hand armed smuggling vessels could be much more formidable and in 1779 the *Norwich Mercury*, April 6th, reported that the smuggling vessels had begun to arm themselves against the revenue cutters on the coasts of Norfolk and Suffolk. The report stated that one of the Yarmouth excise cutters had been resisted when her men were trying to board a free-trading lugger. The smugglers aimed their guns at the King's boats and threatened to fire into them if the officers attempted to board her.

After a prize had been taken it was sent into port by its captors and the crew interned. The vessel and its cargo were eventually sold by auction and the proceeds shared out among the crew of the vessel which made the seizure. In June 1795 it was decreed in a royal warrant what proportion of the prize money each member of a vessel should receive.

Commander	44%
Mate	22%
Deputy Mariner	9% exclusive of his share as a mariner
Other Mariners	25%

Concern was expressed by the Board of Customs that the commanders and crews of revenue cutters would be more interested in prize money than tackling smugglers, and urged the commanders not to leave their stations or neglect their preventive duties when on the lookout for prizes.

The *Lively* excise cutter was stationed at Great Yarmouth for about ten years prior to 1801, when she was transferred to another station. She made quite a number of seizures while she was at the port, and much of the credit for her success was due to her captain, Matthew Gunthorpe, a very efficient officer. Two notable seizures were reported, the first in October 1793 when she took two smuggling boats, the joint cargoes of which amounted to 160 casks of geneva and 3,000 lbs. of tobacco. The second was in April the following year when she seized 5 carts and 6 horses loaded with 310 casks of spirits, 10 cwt. of tobacco and 48 silk handkerchiefs.

However, as it was wartime, she was sometimes called upon to carry out duties other than those connected with smuggling. In 1797, it was reported that a French corvette with 10 guns had captured several English vessels in the North Sea. In September, the *Lively* went to sea to search for some of those prizes. Eventually she sighted and recaptured three brigs, which she escorted into port.

The following year it was reported that Captain Gunthorpe and the crew of the *Lively* cutter, the tide surveyor and the men of the excise boat, supervisors and officers within the Norwich collection, had voluntarily contributed £66 11s. 6d. for the defence of the country, which was paid into the Bank of England.

About 1801 the *Lively* left the Great Yarmouth station and Captain Gunthorpe became the Commander of the *Viper* excise cutter. Many naval vessels had impressed smugglers aboard and they were considered an asset because of their seamanship and fighting qualities. A prize was therefore offered by the Admiralty to the revenue vessel transferring the most smugglers to the Navy in one year. The quality of Captain Gunthorpe's leadership was shown in 1801 when the *Viper* transferred 30 men to the Navy and took the prize of £500.

Captain Gunthorpe eventually retired from the Excise service to reside in a large house on Church Plain in Great Yarmouth. He spent much of his retirement collecting pictures, on which he became an expert.

It appears that there were two customs cutters named *Hunter* stationed at Yarmouth at different times between 1776 and 1807. The first, built in 1775, was a 63-ton vessel with an armament of eight carriage guns and a crew of eighteen men. This vessel was under the command of Captain Fisher. Her earliest reported seizure took place in January 1776, when she took 122 half-ankers of geneva on the beach near Horsey Gap.

Some other incidents involving this vessel and Captain Fisher have already been mentioned, but by February 1786 she was commanded by Captain Timothy Steward. The *Norwich Mercury* reported eight seizures made by the *Hunter* in that year, two of which were off Happisburgh. The first took place on May 18th when one of the *Hunter*'s boats took a smuggling lugger carrying 459 half-ankers of foreign spirits, and some bags of tobacco. As soon as the *Hunter*'s men boarded the lugger the smugglers cut her cable and she was driven on to the beach where she was wrecked. The other seizure took place in August when she took a smuggling cutter laden with 25 half-ankers of foreign spirits, 150 bottles of wine, 61 bags of tobacco, 4 boxes of starch, 1 box of hair powder and 12 bags of currants.

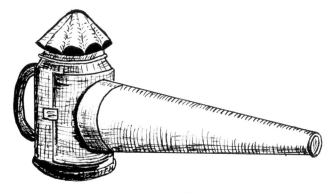

Smuggler's signalling lantern.
This lantern was held in the crook of the left arm while the right hand was placed over the end of the spout through which the light shone. When the spout was pointing seaward the light could only be seen from the sea.

In 1788 Captain Thomas Riches took over command of the *Hunter* and it was under his command, five years later, that two of her crew were killed. On July 25th, 1793, the *Hunter* encountered a smuggling lugger in Southwold Bay. A fierce battle took place in which John Davey and Thomas Cousins were seriously wounded. The men were eventually taken ashore where they died within a few hours of each other. They were given a double funeral.

In their eagerness to catch smuggling boats, some captains of revenue vessels put their own men in danger. This happened on May 16th 1792. It was reported that the Yarmouth customs cutter, which must have been the *Hunter* as she was the only customs cutter at the port, was at sea chasing a smuggling vessel when both boats were becalmed. The customs cutter lowered a six-oared boat, crewed by seven men and the cutter's mate, Mr Manners. As the boat was rowing towards the smuggler, the wind speed suddenly increased. The customs cutter immediately resumed the chase, sailing past its own boat and out of sight of Mr Manners and his men. The mate and the seven men were four days and three nights in the boat before they were picked up by a Swedish snow, a small brig-like vessel with a supplementary trisail mast. They were eventually landed at Elsinore in Denmark on May 23rd. Three of the men, Thomas Watt, Peter Daniel and John Windsel, died from exposure, but the mate and the other four recovered. There was no evidence that an enquiry took place into the circumstances in which these men died and Captain Riches remained in command of the *Hunter.*

It is not known exactly when the second and larger *Hunter* replaced the older vessel, but she was a much more formidable cutter of 143 tons, armed with 14 guns and crewed by 32 men. It is likely that the larger *Hunter* replaced the original vessel during the French wars.

On April 15th 1794, the *Hunter* made use of her letters of marque when she seized the *Mary,* an American brig, commanded by one Titcomb. She was carrying a cargo of wheat, barley and beans, from Bremen, with dispatches for Liverpool. At the same time she took into Yarmouth 150 casks of foreign spirits, which she had seized while cruising.

In 1805 the *Hunter* was on a cruise when she came upon a Danish vessel with a cargo of geneva. This vessel was not a smuggler, but she was boarded by a party from the *Hunter.* They found her papers to be in order, but removed some of her geneva for their own use. A complaint was later made by the Danes and the *Hunter*'s captain and mate were dismissed.

On Wednesday February 18th 1807, the *Hunter* was cruising off Happisburgh under the command of her newly-appointed captain, Thomas Jay. At 3 o'clock in the morning she was caught in a fierce north-easterly gale and blown into shallow water, with her stern facing the cliff. She was wrecked and her captain, mate and crew of thirty-one men were all lost. Three of her crew had been fortunate enough not to be on board. One, Francis Wright, had arrived half an hour too late when she had sailed from Yarmouth the previous Saturday, another was sick and the third was on business in London. Captain Jay left a widow and five young children.

Bad weather also posed problems for smuggling vessels and it was reported in February 1799 that a smuggling vessel with her entire crew had perished in a gale, while attempting to get into Orford Haven on the Suffolk coast.

The Excise Cutter *Resolution* in 1800.
By kind permission of H. M. Customs and Excise

In January 1803 a King's Lynn vessel called the *Hope,* laden with 120 half-ankers of foreign spirits was blown into Yarmouth in distress by an easterly gale. She had been lashed by heavy seas and her master washed overboard. The vessel was immediately seized by customs officers and the spirits lodged in their warehouse.

Between 1804-9, most of the seizures reported in the *Norwich Mercury* and *Norfolk Chronicle* were made by His Majesty's warships. Perhaps the most significant report, February 1st 1806, involved HMS *Cruizer,* commanded by Captain Stoddart. While at sea she sighted 28 smuggling vessels laden with spirits. She had seized between 6 and 16 of these vessels, three of which had already arrived at Yarmouth. This shows the large numbers of vessels bringing contraband into the country. In May that year, the *Cruizer* seized a large lugger in the Calm near the Firth, laden with 612 ankers of geneva, and in July another carrying over 960 tubs of geneva.

It was reported in the *Norwich Mercury,* May 5th 1804, that the Admiralty had issued orders that all persons concerned with smuggling in any way, were to be impressed, notwithstanding any protection they might have and they were not to be discharged on any account afterwards.

This did not deter people from smuggling at sea, or on land, as the profits were so large that they considered the risk worthwhile. However, the smugglers on a Lowestoft vessel were not so lucky. It was reported from Deal in Kent on October 11th 1807 that this vessel had been seized off the French coast by the *Seagull* sloop, a warship. She was laden with 300 kegs of contraband spirits, which were landed there. The smugglers were put on board the *Seagull.*

One of the most interesting smugglers to be captured was Tom Johnson. He was born in Hampshire and when he grew up he became a smuggler. He was twice imprisoned for smuggling and each time he managed to escape. After his second escape, he went to France where he took up smuggling again. Napoleon heard of Johnson's exploits and tried to persuade him to pilot warships across the Channel when he decided to invade England. Johnson refused and was put in prison, where he spent nine months before he escaped. He made his way to America and the following report appeared in the *Norwich Mercury* in August 1804.

'On Sunday sailed the *Mermaid* revenue cutter with a person on board, reported to be Johnson, the noted smuggler, as he answers to the description given of him. He was found secreted on board a vessel brought in here by the *Repulse* revenue cutter, a few days ago. The vessel had been detained some hours before he had been discovered. He was sent on board the Admiral's ship, where he was examined, and on him was found an American pass for six months, two of which are expired.'

Johnson was pardoned and for several years he distinguished himself while serving as a pilot in His Majesty's Navy. After the war he became the captain of a revenue cutter called the *Fox,* before he retired on a pension.

Cawston, a wholesale dealer in spirits, appeared before the Lord Chief Baron in the Exchequer Court on July 7th 1808, charged with smuggling. Several times he had run contraband on the Norfolk coast in his cutter. The Crown hoped to recover penalties on certain quantities of brandy, rum and geneva smuggled into Norfolk from

Flushing and other Dutch ports. The Crown's informants were some of Cawston's customers and a smuggler who had worked for him.

The Solicitor-General, for the prosecution, described Cawston as a wholesale dealer in illegal traffic to a considerable extent. He was known to have taken charge of four cargoes smuggled into Norfolk between the harvest of 1805 and the end of 1806. The *Norwich Mercury* claimed that the Crown had acted in this case with unmerited clemency by not asking for the double value of the goods, as it was entitled to do, but a reduced single value of 10s. per gallon. The actual value was 16s. and 18s. per gallon. Instead of estimating each cargo at 2,000 gallons they limited them to 500 gallons each. 'The jury found a verdict of £250, the single value of the geneva and brandy, no rum being sworn to.'

During this trial, the defence argued that the informers were not entitled to credit as the seaman was not only a smuggler but a deserter from the Navy, and the others had knowingly purchased smuggled spirits. The Lord Chief Baron replied that if one of the informers had abandoned the service of the country, a strong inducement to his doing so had been held out by the defendant himself. He had paid him £8 a trip, which might last a fortnight, whereas in the Navy he was only paid 5s. per month. It was principally through the information of the parties concerned that this very serious offence had been detected and such persons therefore were not to be esteemed incompetent witnesses. The £8 per trip paid to the seaman indicates the great value of smuggled goods at this time.

During the war with France, Napoleon realised that the English smugglers could be used to his advantage. He encouraged them by fitting up the port of Roscoff as a refuge for them, allowing them to purchase goods cheaply, to sell in England at a large profit. In return Napoleon wanted the free traders to smuggle his spies into England and to carry letters for him. The smugglers were so well paid for their trouble that many of them were unpatriotic enough to comply with his wishes. It has also been said that the smugglers took English spies into France.

Napoleon had another reason for assisting English smugglers, and that was gold. Gold was very valuable in France as French credit was so low that his Spanish troops would only accept gold as payment for their services. Provided the smugglers paid for their spirits with gold, the French would sell to them very cheaply. Although the export of gold from England was prohibited, great quantities were taken out of the country by the smugglers. This was now two-way smuggling; guineas were being exported and spirits imported. Eventually gold became so scarce in England that restrictions were placed on its use.

An attempt to smuggle gold out of the country was reported in the *Norwich Mercury*, December 7th 1810. Elias Loveday, the Yarmouth tide surveyor, rummaged a vessel at the port and discovered 22 bars of gold weighing 2,370 ounces. He found the metal cunningly concealed between the vessel's timbers under about 30 tons of shingle ballast.

Much of the contraband taken by the revenue officers was sold at auctions held at the Yarmouth Excise Office or the Custom House. A sale by auction to be held at the former on November 27th 1804 was advertised in the *Norwich Mercury*. This sale consisted of 1,000 gallons of geneva, for private use only, and about 90 gallons of brandy for dealers and others. These were to be sold in small lots for the convenience of the public.

The following advertisement appeared in the *Norwich Mercury*, January 10th 1807, and shows the variety of goods sold at these sales.

'To Be Sold By Auction.
At the Customs House, Great Yarmouth, on Tuesday, 27th day of January 1807, at Two o'clock in the afternoon in small lots.
For Private Use.
About 1000 Gallons of Geneva
673 Pairs of Angola Gloves
132 Bottles of Hælem Drops
35 Yards of Long Lawn
300 Yards of Black Crepe
5 cwt, 2 qr 6 lbs of Rope
0 cwt, 1 qr 9 lbs of Feathers
2 cwt 2 qr 6 lbs of Tea
112 Deal Ends.
7 Flag Stones and a Rocking Horse
For Exportation
358 Pairs of Leather Gloves

The whole of which may be viewed and tasted, by applying at the place of sale the morning previous thereto.'

Great Yarmouth.
From 1802 until recent years this building was used
as the Custom House.

6. The Preventive Waterguard and Coastguard

The Revenue forces were reorganised when the Preventive Waterguard was established in 1809. The coastline was divided into three districts, Norfolk coming into the third, which extended from London to Berwick. The districts were sub-divided into stations, each of which was manned by a chief officer, chief boatman, two commissioned boatmen and four ordinary boatmen. The stations were provided with a sailing and rowing galley. The boatmen were paid £5 per annum and 3s. a day when employed, and the chief boatman £15 per annum and 4s. a day when employed. The new force was under the command of a Comptroller-General, who was a naval officer, and the men recruited were mainly former sailors. The Preventive Waterguard was expected to operate in coastal waters and search for smugglers who had slipped past the revenue and naval vessels, which patrolled further out to sea. The Waterguard was also expected to carry out shore patrols and to assist the riding officers when necessary. There was a reward of £20 for every smuggler captured and the crew shared in the value of the goods they seized.

Six inspecting generals were appointed to supervise the riding officers in their areas and provide better co-operation with the Waterguard. The duty of the riding officers, or Landguard as they were called, was to collect intelligence concerning smuggling activities which could be used to assist their colleagues afloat, act as links between the boat stations and to intercept inland contraband that had been successfully run on the coast.

Some of the many seizures made by the preventive boats stationed in the towns and villages on the Norfolk coast were reported in the *Norwich Mercury* at this time. A typical report was made on October 16th 1811, concerning the Mundesley preventive boat. The sitter, as the chief boatman was called, and crew seized an open smuggling lugger near the shore, carrying 250 casks of geneva and about 100 casks of brandy. They took the lugger into Blakeney Harbour and the spirits were deposited in the customs warehouse at Cley.

Smuggling continued to be rife on the Norfolk coast and this was shown by the following extract from the *Norwich Mercury*, February 29th 1812. 'A few evenings since, the cargoes of five smuggling

The Coastguard Station at Thornham in 1924.

vessels were seized on the Norfolk coast'. Some smuggling cargoes were quite substantial and the following January the Sheringham preventive boat was reported to have captured a smuggling cutter off Salthouse, laden with 600 casks of geneva. This vessel and her cargo were also taken to Blakeney and the spirits deposited in the warehouse at Cley.

The Preventive Waterguard and the revenue cruisers were expected to co-operate with each other and in May 1815 an example of this took place, involving the *Tiger* cutter and the Sheringham preventive boat. They seized a smuggling vessel at sea called the *Pitt* of Folkestone and split her cargo between them. The preventive boat took 90 half-ankers of geneva into Cley while the *Tiger* took the vessel and the remainder of the cargo into Yarmouth.

What effect did the conclusion of the war with France have on smuggling and the Revenue services in 1815? When the war with France ended, the Navy had control of the seas and many naval vessels were utilised to protect the Revenue; others were paid off and their crews transferred to the Waterguard. Smuggling vessels could no longer rely on their guns to see them safely to their destinations and speed and secrecy became the priorities for craft running contraband.

An armed three-masted Smuggling Lugger.
Re-drawn from an illustration in *Once upon a Tide* by Hervey Benham

With the return of peace, many soldiers and sailors were discharged from the services and the Government thought that many of these men, who had fought in many parts of Europe, would not adapt to civilian life very easily and might turn to smuggling. To combat this, the number of preventive boats around the coasts was increased and entry to the Waterguard became dependant on age and experience. All new recruits had to be between twenty-five and thirty-five years of age with six years' experience at sea, or have served a seven-year apprenticeship with a fisherman. Just how strictly they kept to the ages specified is not known, but younger men did enter the service - perhaps they lied about their age.

In 1816 the laws for the prevention of smuggling were strengthened. It was now illegal for a rowing boat to have more than four oars and any discovered with more than four was subject to forfeit; her oarsmen faced fines of £40 each. If any illegal rowing galleys used by the smugglers were seized they were usually cut in half. Vessels with more than four oars had to be specially licensed and boatbuilders were forbidden to build luggers of more than 50 tons.

These changes did not deter the smugglers on the east coast. The following extract from the *Norwich Mercury*, March 16th 1816, concerning several seizures made on the north Norfolk coast, indicates the regularity with which smuggled goods were being run and the success of the revenue forces.

'On Tuesday sevennight were seized at Weybourne, 30 half-ankers of foreign Geneva. On Wednesday were picked up off Blakeney, 26 half-ankers ditto, and one open tub-boat and Thursday, in the parishes of Sydestrand and Overstrand, 126 half-ankers ditto, which were all conveyed to Blakeney and deposited in the King's warehouse'.

Since it was very important for smugglers to get as much speed out of their craft as possible, the Government passed a law aimed at reducing the speed of smuggling vessels. Under an Act passed in 1817, it was illegal for any vessel to carry a bowsprit of more than two-thirds the length of its hull; any craft not complying with this law would be seized. The shorter bowsprit had the effect of reducing a vessel's speed. But the Act did not apply to revenue cutters, whose bowsprits were often almost as long as their hulls to give them extra speed. At this time revenue cutters were clinker-built, lapped planking. They were strongly constructed, with a heavy mast and a large sail. Their armament usually consisted of about twelve carriage guns, several swivel guns and a crew of about twenty men armed with pistols, muskets and cutlasses. Revenue cutters put to sea in all weathers and, although life on board was very hard, there was no shortage of recruits for the service. Men serving on board these vessels were issued with certificates that exempted them from being impressed into the Navy.

Foreign luggers were often employed, carrying mixed crews consisting of either English and Dutch men or English and French men. This was because no alien could be charged with an offence committed outside his country's territorial waters. A lucrative seizure was made by the Mundesley preventive boat of a cargo and smugglers in December 1816, when she chased and took an open smuggling vessel laden with 415 half-ankers of brandy and geneva. The smugglers, consisting of four English and three Dutchmen, were taken prisoner. Later the English were put on board a cutter and the Dutchmen were released.

This situation existed for a number of years. In June 1825 HMS

Brisk, a sloop, arrived in Yarmouth harbour carrying six smugglers, 40 half-ankers of spirits, 5 casks of tobacco and one of snuff. It was reported that two of the men 'being Englishmen' were sent to prison. Another case was in September that year, when a large tub boat with seven foreigners and one Englishman on board was taken off Warham by the crew of the Preventive boat at Morston. Her cargo consisted of 198 half-ankers of geneva, 17 half-ankers of brandy, 22 casks of tobacco, 1 cask of tea and a box of playing cards.

With the increased strength and efficiency of the post-war revenue forces, their patrols ashore and at sea were stepped up and smugglers running their goods stood a greater chance of being intercepted. This meant that they had to exercise more care, cunning and ingenuity when going about their business. It was the usual practice for a smuggling vessel to unload its cargo on the beach, or lay off the shore while tub boats ferried the cargo to the beach. These methods of unloading, however, took time, which increased the chances of discovery. This led to the smugglers adopting a practice that took much less time. They began weighting tubs with sinking stones, sailing close to the shore and dumping them overboard, attached to a recovery line. The other end of the line was fixed to a buoy on, or close to, the surface. This method of concealment was known as 'sowing the crop'; the tubs could be collected later when the coast was clear.

This ploy was quite successful, but it did have its weaknesses, as severe storms could sometimes drive the tubs ashore. It was also common practice on the east coast for men to try to salvage lost anchors. They would drag hooks from a boat along the seabed in the hope of picking them up, but sometimes they brought a crop of tubs to the surface instead. In 1819, near Pakefield on the Suffolk coast, a beach boat dragging for anchors came upon 112 casks of brandy and gin, which were taken to the customs warehouse at Great Yarmouth.

Smugglers on all the coasts of England sank tubs in the sea when it suited their purpose. In May 1824, W. Cater, an excise officer in Leiston, Suffolk, discovered 113 half-ankers of gin sunk off Aldeburgh. They were lashed to a cable and sunk in about three fathoms of water. They were held in position by four small anchors. The officer seized them and sent them to the excise office at Saxmundham.

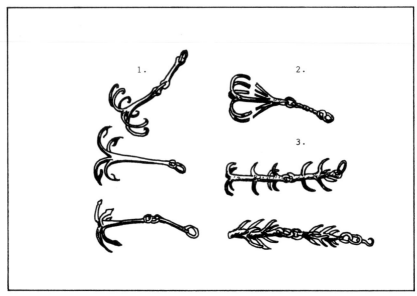

Creepers. These were dragged along the sea-bed to bring sunken goods to the surface. 1. Sand creepers 2. Rock creeper 3.Centipedes.

To combat this form of concealment the preventive men used to carry out creeping and sweeping patrols. Creeping consisted of dragging a grapnel, or creep as it was called, along the seabed to hook on to submerged tubs. While sweeping, two boats were rowed along, parallel to each other, dragging a bight, a loop of rope, between them along the bottom. It was hard work but when successful could prove lucrative for the boatmen.

Some Norfolk smugglers made use of this method of hiding their goods on the county's inland waterways, such as the Broads, rivers and dikes. Brighton Silvers, the Customs Tide Surveyor at Yarmouth, and his boatmen made two seizures of smuggled goods hidden in this manner. A tide surveyor was the officer in charge of a boarding or rummage crew. However, the places and circumstances in which he made some of his seizures show that he was prepared to go well beyond the duties of his office to seize contraband. Some of his most notable seizures took place inland, well away from Yarmouth. His first reported seizure was made eleven miles north west of the port, one night in March 1817 when, with four of his boatmen, he discovered 81 tubs of geneva submerged in South Walsham Broad.

Silvers was a very able officer, making seizures inland, on the

A method used by smugglers to sink a crop of tubs containing spirits.
Re-drawn from an illustration in *Smuggling* by David Phillipson

beaches and at sea. In November 1817, it took the combined efforts of Silvers, Martin, also a tide surveyor at Yarmouth, their boatmen and the *Tartar* cutter to take a Dutch open lugger laden with about 300 tubs of spirits on the North Beach at Yarmouth. Two years later, in April, Silvers and his men made the first of two inland seizures west of Yarmouth. They were searching some ditches in the parish of Runham when they discovered submerged in them 41 half-ankers of geneva, containing 150 gallons. The other seizure took place on the turnpike road leading to Yarmouth in January the following year, when they took a horse and cart loaded with 24 half-ankers of geneva.

On the night of May 30th 1823, Silvers and his crew were on duty at Yarmouth when a large, open, smuggling lugger made a dash through the harbour and into Breydon Water. Silvers and his men manned their boat and chased the lugger, rowing strongly until they overtook her just before she reached the River Yare. Her cargo consisted of 165 casks of gin and brandy, 99 casks and packages of tobacco, 40 casks of tea and some other goods. All the smugglers, except for one man, made their escape.

Later that year, on Friday September 19th, the *De Hoop* of Middelburg arrived in Yarmouth Harbour from Bruges. Silvers decided to rummage her and after examining her carefully, he found over 1,000 lbs of manufactured tobacco concealed in various places.

South Walsham Broad.
In March 1817 customs officers discovered eighty-one tubs
of geneva submerged in the Broad.

Two Dutchmen found on board, Jan Heybeck and Andres Saiffart, were committed to Yarmouth gaol; the rest of the crew escaped.

The Yarmouth preventive boat was also active and in April 1820 she was reported to have made a seizure of 116 half-ankers of geneva. However, six months later she was involved in a tragedy on the River Bure. Edward Blake, the chief boatman, and his men were sailing up the river very early one morning in October. After travelling about four miles a sudden squall of wind caused the sail to gibe and upset the boat. Mr Blake was drowned, but his boatmen were saved.

For many years Kentish smuggling vessels had run cargoes on the east coast, sometimes as far north as Yorkshire. It must have been worthwhile for these smugglers to have contacts in the north and it may have been easier to run their cargoes well away from the Kent coast, where they were less likely to be caught. However, it was in 1817 that the 'coast blockade' was established to guard the coasts of Kent and Sussex, where smuggling had been going on for many years on an immense scale. The new force came under the control of the Admiralty and was stationed between North Foreland and New-haven. It was under the command of Captain William McCulloch, a strict disciplinarian nicknamed by his men 'Flogging Joey'. The blockade depended on men going ashore at sunset and patrolling the shore at night, returning to their ships at dawn. There was no Preventive Waterguard in this area.

Apart from the coast blockade, the Navy provided ships and men for revenue duties. Sixty-nine naval vessels were assisting the revenue in 1819. The Board of Customs had its own fleet, and the Preventive Waterguard and the Board of Excise launched seven cutters. In addition to this, there were fifty-six sloops and other vessels patrolling British waters.

HMS *Florida,* commanded by Captain Hawthyne, was stationed at Great Yarmouth in 1818. On May 11th she was cruising in the Straits of Dover, when Captain Hawthyne sent Keith Stewart, master's mate, out on patrol in one of the *Florida*'s boats, with orders to intercept any suspicious boats coming from the French coast. After several hours on patrol, Stewart came upon a large galley under sail and oars off Calais. When he closed with her, he discovered she was the *St Thomas* of Deal. Stewart ordered her commander to lower her sails, but he merely ordered his men to row faster. The officer then warned him that he would open fire if he did not heave to. Back came the reply from the galley, 'Fire and be damned'. Stewart, however, held his fire, and his men pulled alongside the galley. His boatmen attempted to grapple her gunwhale with his boathook, but it was promptly knocked aside.

Stewart, however, leapt aboard the galley, followed by his coxswain, and her steersman aimed a pistol at him. The officer fired first and the man fell to the deck. At that moment the *Florida*'s boat and the galley drifted apart, leaving the two officers to face a hostile crew, which had crowded aft. Drawing his sword, Stewart ordered the men forward, and immediately two of them rushed at him and he slashed them both. The remainder of the crew then backed off and when Stewart's men clambered aboard they surrendered. The galley was a smuggler laden with 207 casks of tobacco and 100 of tea. She was carrying a mixed crew of seven Englishmen, three of whom were wounded, and six Dutchmen. Before they arrived back at Yarmouth, one of the wounded, said to be the skipper, had died. The account of this action in the *Norwich Mercury,* May 16th 1818, varied in some details from the above account, stating that she was the *St Thomas* of Dunkirk with eleven hands on board, four of whom were wounded and that one had since died. The report also maintained that she was carrying 270 casks of tobacco. An entry in St Nicholas' church register made on May 17th, when the dead seaman was buried, showed that he was a Yarmouth man, 'Richard Woodham smuggler (shot) of Yarmouth'.

It was possible for men to transfer between the different branches of the Revenue Service. Robert Waller, a deputy mariner aboard the *Hawk* revenue cutter, was appointed to the post of chief officer on the preventive boat at Kessingland on the Suffolk coast, just south of Great Yarmouth. While carrying out his duties aboard the *Hawk*, he was responsible, in September 1815, for the seizure of the forty-six-ton smuggling sloop, *Prosperous*, William Suggett, her master, and her cargo of 400 casks of spirits and a small quantity of tobacco.

An important seizure he made while in charge of the preventive boat was reported in the newspapers in March 1820, when he took a large smuggling vessel, the *De Hoop*, on the beach at Kessingland. She was laden with over 100 tubs of spirits and several bales of hand-kerchiefs. Three of the five-man crew escaped, but the other two, numb with cold after so long at sea, were captured. An unusual aspect of this seizure was that when the cargo was taken into Yarmouth the liquor was deposited in the excise warehouse and the handkerchiefs in the customs warehouse.

During the years 1813-1816, several revenue cutters were operating from Great Yarmouth. This was shown in a report in the *Norwich Mercury*, October 7th 1815, which stated 'Sailed the *Hardy* sloop of war and three revenue cutters on a cruise'. The cutters were the *Hawk*, *Repulse* and *Industry* and there were several reports of the seizures they made at this time. Eventually these cutters were replaced by the *Ranger* and *Tartar*.

The *Ranger* customs cutter was commanded by Captain John Sayers. She had fourteen guns and carried a crew of twenty-nine men and three boys, although crew numbers on revenue vessels varied from time to time. Several reports of seizures made by this cutter appear in the *Norwich Mercury*. In December 1811, she captured a lugger laden with 909 tubs of spirits, and three years later she seized a sloop-rigged smuggler in the Swin, in the Thames estuary, laden with over 300 casks of spirits. The crew, who attempted to escape in a boat, were taken prisoner and put on board a guard ship. Another report in January 1816 stated that she sent into Yarmouth two smuggling sloops, the *Cossack* and the *Duke of Wellington*, with cargoes amounting to 940 casks of geneva and dry goods.

On March 19th 1817, the *Ranger* was involved in a fierce sea battle lasting one and a half hours with the *Folkestone* of Folkestone, a large smuggling lugger carrying thirty-six men and armed with twelve nine-pounder guns and nine muskets. The *Ranger* came upon her off the Yorkshire coast near Robin Hood's Bay, about 9 o'clock in the evening. She immediately fired a warning shot across the lugger's bows to bring her to for boarding. However, the *Folkestone* returned her fire and the battle began. Eventually the smugglers decided to abandon their vessel and under the cover of darkness they slipped away in their boats, leaving the badly-damaged lugger with two dead men on board. Other casualties suffered by the smugglers were unknown, but the *Ranger* had three men killed and seven wounded, four seriously.

The bodies of the three men killed were returned to Yarmouth and conveyed to the Wrestlers Inn on Church Plain. They were Joseph Boston, aged thirty-three years, John Palmer aged twenty-four years and Charles Wigg aged twenty-three years. Silent crowds witnessed the funeral of these men, which took place on Sunday 23rd March at St Nicholas' Church. The coffins were conveyed from the inn to the church by men from the crew of the *Tartar* cutter. The procession was led by the parish beadles, a number of the *Ranger*'s crew, two by two, William Palgrave and John Preston, the Collector and Comptroller of the Customs at Yarmouth, Captain Sayers and Lieutenant Claxton. The flag on the church flew at half-mast and the *Tartar* fired two-minute guns during the ceremony. The two smugglers were buried in St Nicholas' churchyard the following day and the entry in the church register merely states, 'Buried two men unknown from a smuggling cutter'.

It was known that the *Folkestone* was making her sixth trip which suggests that the *Ranger* was on the lookout for her. Her cargo consisted of 507 ankers and 945 half-ankers of spirits, 27 bales of tobacco, 206 bags of tea, 47 bales of silk handkerchiefs, 9 boxes of playing cards and some cordials. Estimates of the value of the ship and cargo varied from over £9,000 to £13,000.

Smugglers usually made every effort to escape when their vessels and goods were taken by revenue officers. They knew that if they were captured they could be impressed into the Navy. A smuggling vessel was seized by the *Ranger* off Yarmouth in April 1821 between the Old Jetty and the Nelson Monument. She was carrying 400 tubs of geneva, but her crew made their escape by jumping overboard and swimming ashore.

Sometimes, when smugglers were captured, they could be difficult to secure and would make as much trouble for their captors as possible. The *Susannah,* a large smuggling lugger with a crew of thirty-four men, was seized by the *Ranger* in June 1822, after a twelve-hour chase in which one smuggler was killed and another wounded. Eleven of the smuggler's crew were captured and taken into Yarmouth where they were held in the town gaol. It was decided to transport them to Chatham on board the *Ranger,* where they would be put on board a man of war. To avoid trouble from the local population the eleven men were to be removed from Yarmouth gaol at 2 o'clock one morning, but when the officers arrived at the prison, the smugglers threatened to fight to the death rather than allow themselves to be removed. The officers therefore decided to wait for reinforcements from the *Ranger,* and the smugglers were eventually removed later that morning. As the smugglers and their escort made their way to the beach, they were followed by a large crowd of people. The officers were jeered and pelted with stones, and had great difficulty in getting the prisoners on board the *Ranger* and preventing them from being rescued. When the *Ranger*'s boats returned to the jetty to pick up Captain Sayers, they were again attacked by the crowd still assembled there, and two of the crew were severely wounded. Six of the attackers were arrested and committed to prison. The eleven smugglers were eventually put on board HMS *Genoa,* at Sheerness and on account of their violent behaviour they were all put in irons.

It was in October 1822 that the *Ranger* made her last cruise from Yarmouth, which was to end in tragedy. On the night of Sunday 13th, while she was at sea off Happisburgh and two of her boats were away looking for smugglers, a severe gale suddenly blew up from the north east. One of the boats with seven men on board was unable to return to the *Ranger,* so she put in at Cromer. It is not known whether the other boat overturned or managed to reach her for, like many other vessels that night, the *Ranger* was wrecked and all thirty men on board, including Captain Sayers and Mr Ballard, the first mate, were drowned. Since everybody on board died, no account of exactly what happened was available. The following morning, the wreck was washed ashore with the body of Mr Ballard. The bodies of several

Happisburgh. Villagers were accused of making no attempt to rescue the crew of the *Ranger* customs cutter when she was wrecked in 1822.

other crew members were later picked up, but not that of Captain Sayers. The *Ranger* was said to have been wrecked within one hundred and fifty yards of the spot where the *Hunter* was lost fifteen years earlier.

Allegations were made that the people of Happisburgh made no attempt to rescue the crew of the *Ranger* and shamefully neglected her signals of distress. 'The shrieks of the crew', it was said, 'were heard distinctly on the shore, yet no attempt was made to rescue'. These allegations were strongly denied by the inhabitants of Happisburgh, but it did not pass unnoticed that they expressed no regret at the tragedy.

The other revenue cutter stationed at Great Yarmouth was the *Tartar*, commanded by Captain Worthington. In 1815 she seized two Yarmouth vessels, at sea, with contraband on board. The first, taken in March, was the *Benjamin,* an open boat laden with 150 half-ankers of geneva and a quantity of tobacco. She was seized near Lowestoft by boats belonging to the *Tartar.* The other, taken the following month, was the *Persis,* an open lugger with a cargo of 144 tubs of geneva, which was seized by the *Tartar* in Yarmouth Roads. Both cargoes were deposited in the customs' warehouse in Yarmouth.

The *Tartar* operated from the Great Yarmouth station for about eight years. In her latter years at the port she was commanded by Lieutenant Woolnough. She was smaller than the *Ranger* and this was reflected in the size of the vessels and cargoes she seized. The biggest seizure reported in the Norfolk newspapers that involved the *Tartar* was a Dutch open lugger laden with 300 tubs of spirits on the north beach at Yarmouth. However this seizure was a combined effort between the *Tartar*'s crew and two Yarmouth tide surveyors, Martin and Silvers, and their boatmen.

In theory the revenue cutters were to patrol some distance from the coast, leaving the coastal waters to be patrolled by the preventive boats. However, this was ignored by the cutters, who often operated close to the shore and sent their boats to search the beaches and creeks for smugglers. In January 1816, a smuggling sloop from Maasluys was at anchor in Corton Roads, south of Yarmouth. She had a cargo of spirits, tobacco, plate glass (in illegal packages) and playing cards. Joseph Ballard, a deputy mariner from the *Ranger*, seized the vessel on the beach, with her cargo and three carts and two horses, which were being used to carry goods inland.

At times fierce skirmishes took place between the smugglers and revenue officers. One night in March 1816, a smuggling vessel landed a cargo of contraband on the beach at Caister, just north of Yarmouth. Information concerning the running of this cargo had been received by Customs and Excise at Yarmouth. Several officers from both services went to Caister and came upon a large party of men in the process of carrying a number of casks, containing foreign spirits, from the beach. A serious affray took place between the officers and smugglers, which lasted for some time. Eventually the officers seized 125 casks and secured six of the ringleaders. The officers had been badly bruised and cut by the men throwing large stones at them and Mr Toby, the Supervisor of Excise, was so severely wounded that he had to be carried back to Yarmouth in a cart. He was attended by a surgeon who dressed his wounds but, although out of danger, it was feared he would lose the sight of one eye.

In April, the six smugglers, Wright, Carman, Woodhouse, Hopgood, Mullender and George Dobson the younger appeared before the magistrates and were committed to Norwich Castle. They were charged on the oaths of several witnesses with throwing stones, wounding and obstructing the officers of customs and excise in the course of their duty. At the same time the magistrates issued warrants for the arrest of three other smugglers who had absconded.

On the morning of Tuesday October 7th 1823, a large open lugger called *La Leverette* was on the beach at Winterton with 200 half-ankers of geneva on board. It was not long before three men on duty at the Preventive Station at Winterton came upon the vessel. They were the chief boatman, John Sarwood, James Barton, a commissioned boatman, and James Sneller, a boatman. The officers seized the lugger and her cargo, but not without fierce resistance from over forty smugglers armed with bludgeons. They attacked the officers violently, knocking Sarwood and Barton to the ground, and began beating them savagely. The officers then fired their pistols in self-defence and severely wounded several of the smugglers, who all made their escape. In November, the Customs Commissioners offered a reward of £50 to anybody giving information that led to the conviction of any one, or more, of the smugglers. The reward was to be paid by the Collector of the Customs at Yarmouth.

In February 1833, early on the morning of the 26th, the Weybourne riding officer and a boatman were patrolling together. A terrier, belonging to the officer, pushed through a hedge into a field and began barking excitedly. The two men, thinking the dog was after a hare or rabbit, went to investigate and saw a man with an umbrella and a stick whom they took to be a scout for a smuggling party. Almost immediately, a number of smugglers arrived on the scene and the riding officer attempted to fire his pistol to alert the coastguard, but it misfired. One of the smugglers pointed a gun at him and threatened to kill him if he tried to raise the alarm again. The smugglers then handcuffed the officer's hands behind him and went about their business. Meanwhile the boatman had run for help and alerted the chief officer, Lieutenant Howes, at the watch house, who with another man went in search of the smugglers.

They soon came upon a horseless cart, partly loaded with contraband, which had been deliberately left by the smugglers in the hope that the officers would be content to seize it and give up their pursuit. However, the officers continued to follow the smugglers and soon caught up with them. The smugglers, said to number over a hundred, had 20 to 30 carts and horses, some empty and some loaded. As the officers approached, many of the smugglers fled, leaving between forty and fifty men to fight them off. The two officers attacked the smugglers, who hurled stones at them and fought back with bludgeons. The fight lasted for some time, during which Lieutenant Howes broke two of his pistols when he struck several smugglers on their heads. He also ran his dirk through the arm of a smuggler, who escaped with it sticking in his arm, wounded several others with his cutlass and fired a number of shots. Eventually the smugglers were fooled by a false alarm when another officer opened fire as he approached the scene. The coastguard men cheered, implying that reinforcements were coming, and the smugglers panicked and fled in all directions, leaving five loaded horses and carts and two wounded men. One, named Ward of Hempstead, was seriously wounded when a ball passed through both his legs, fracturing the main bones in one of them. This resulted in his leg being amputated later that day. The other man, Pigle from Bacons-thorpe, was slightly wounded. Several other smugglers retreated from the scene with cutlass and pistol-shot wounds.

There were many reports of contraband goods being picked up at sea and the weather was often responsible for this. At times storms wrecked large numbers of vessels on the east coast and some of them were smuggling craft. Several lives were lost in October 1829, when a severe gale occurred off the Norfolk coast; at Brancaster the pre-ventive men picked up 291 casks of brandy and geneva.

In February 1822 many coastal vessels picked up contraband from the sea near Boston Deeps in the Wash, which they took to Yarmouth Custom House. It was thought that a smuggling vessel had been lost in that area, as a pump was also recovered. The cargo rescued amounted to 300 tubs of spirits and several bags of tea and tobacco.

Contraband was also sometimes discovered floating in the sea, after a smuggling craft had been chased by a revenue vessel. To make their vessel lighter the smugglers would throw their cargo overboard. Two instances of this were reported in the *Norwich Mercury*. The first took place in May 1822, when the boats of the *Repulse* cutter were pursuing a smuggling boat and, during the chase, the smugglers threw their entire cargo overboard. Eventually the smugglers beached their vessel at Hemsby and 40 half-ankers of spirits were picked up. The second incident took place three years later, when 271 casks of spirits, several casks of tobacco, boxes of playing cards and other goods were picked up at sea and taken to Yarmouth Custom House. It was thought to have been part of a cargo thrown overboard by a smuggling vessel being pursued by His Majesty's revenue cutters.

The duties of the revenue officers could be unexpectedly hazardous at times. Officers risked injury and death in skirmishes with smugglers, and sometimes their normal patrols and watches could lead to tragedy. A boatman named Linder of the Yarmouth Customs was on watch on the pier at 12 o'clock on the night of February 1st 1823. When it was time for his watch to end there was no sign of him. It was a very dark night and it was thought that he had walked over the side of the pier and drowned.

The sea also claimed victims from the Preventive Service, as shown by a tombstone in the churchyard of All Saints, Morston, on the Norfolk coast.

'Memory
Wm Luce Son of Wm
AND Anna Luce
drowned from a
Preventive boat.
Feb 26th 1834 having a
tender mother to lament
for her only son
Age 22.'

In 1822 the revenue forces were reorganised to promote greater efficiency. The Preventive Waterguard was again placed under the control of the Board of Customs along with the smaller revenue vessels, the larger ones remaining under Admiralty control, and the riding officers were reduced in number to fifty men. The new force was called the Coastguard and its first comptroller-general was Captain William Bowles R.N. Although he was answerable to the Customs Commissioners, all the new recruits appointed to the Coastguard were nominated by the Admiralty. From this date on, the cutters were regarded as a branch of the Coastguard, of which they remained until the second half of the century, when smuggling had appreciably declined.

In March 1823, the Customs Commissioners began to tighten up controls at the ports. They gave notice of a practice that had prevailed among several masters of vessels arriving at ports in the kingdom.

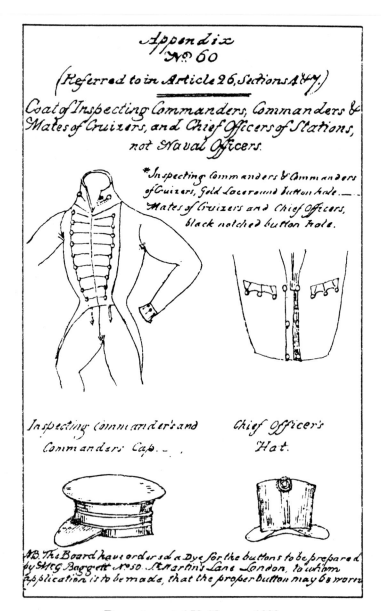

Appendix
Nº 60

(Referred to in Article 26, Sections 4 & 7.)

Coat of Inspecting Commanders, Commanders & Mates of Cruizers, and Chief Officers of Stations, not Naval Officers.

Inspecting Commanders & Commanders of Cruizers, Gold Lace round button hole.—
Mates of Cruizers and Chief Officers, black notched button hole.

Inspecting Commander's and Commanders' Cap.—

Chief Officer's Hat.

N.B. The Board have ordered a Dye for the buttons to be prepared by Mr G Baggett Nº 50 St Martin's Lane London, to whom application is to be made, that the proper button may be worn.

Departmental Uniforms, 1829.
By kind permission of H.M.Customs and Excise

106

These masters did not give correct reports of the cargoes they were carrying, as required by law. For example, instead of inserting on a report the exact number of pieces of timber cut for stowage, the word 'about' was used before the number and this also applied to other items. The Commissioners ruled that in future any master who made an incorrect report of his cargo would be fined £100 and any goods not reported would be seized.

The organisation of the Revenue forces did not impress everyone connected with them. Captain Frederick Marryat R.N.C.B., who spent the last years of his life at the Manor House, Langham, near Holt, was employed on preventive duty in the Channel from 1820 to 1822. He addressed a memorandum to the Admiralty on the inefficiency of the service and suggested improvements. He claimed that the revenue cruisers were dispersed over too wide an area of the coast and spent too much time at anchor; the cruisers would have a better chance of falling in with the smugglers if they were to blockade the ports most frequented by them, such as Cherbourg, Flushing and Roscoff. However, his suggestions were not taken up by the Admiralty.

Looking at the service as a whole, the quality of the men recruited may in part have made the force less effective. During the seven years 1821-27, two hundred and twenty-nine men were dismissed from the service, chiefly for drunkenness, outrageous conduct, insubordination, or connection with smugglers. On dismissal, some offenders actually joined the smugglers.

When ships were wrecked and washed ashore they were often guarded by the Coastguard to prevent looting by the local people. However, the officers sometimes turned a blind eye while the wreckers plundered stricken ships or helped themselves. In November 1835, the *Harriet,* a schooner from St Petersburg, bound for Liverpool, was lost with her eight-man crew off Hunstanton. When the vessel was washed ashore many people appeared on the beach and scrambled among the wreckage, breaking it up and carrying it away unmolested by those present, whose duty it was to prevent such plunder.

It was during a severe gale in February two years later that the sixty-ton *Raby Castle* was driven ashore off Salthouse and became a total wreck. She was bound from London to Stockton with a valuable cargo. The crew and passengers were saved. It was reported that

'When she broke up the beach was strewed with spirits, wine, oranges, nuts, teas, toys, hampers, boxes etc.'. Many men and women arrived on the beach and began helping themselves. One group staved a spirit cask and allowed its contents to run into their oilskin hats, shoes and anything else at hand. Others were seen filling their pockets with handkerchiefs. Many men and women had to be conveyed from the beach 'literally dead drunk'. All this took place before contingents of coastguard men. Many who were charged to guard the property were themselves intoxicated. The cargo of the *Raby Castle* was valued at £5,000 of which about £800 worth was recovered. The wreck was eventually auctioned for £41.

Although it could be argued that not all coastguard men were of the highest integrity, it could also be argued that not all smugglers were completely unprincipled. The seamanship of two captured smugglers proved invaluable to the *Badger* revenue cutter in November 1838. The *Badger*, under the command of Lieut. R. Perceval R.N., came upon the sloop *Volharden* of Flushing at sea, which she seized on suspicion of smuggling. As they made for Yarmouth, the *Badger* got into difficulties, which she managed to overcome with the assistance of two of the smugglers. When they arrived in port, large quantities of spirits were found on board the *Volharden*. On December 7th the smuggler's crew were sentenced to six months' imprisonment by Yarmouth magistrates. Lieut. Perceval recommended two of them to mercy on the grounds that they had assisted the *Badger* when she was in difficulties, and they had their sentences reduced to three months' imprisonment.

At least one person was concerned for the religious and moral welfare of the coastguard men and that was Elizabeth Fry, the Quaker reformer and philanthropist. She was responsible for providing libraries for the five hundred coastguard stations on the shores of Great Britain and the forty-eight cruisers afloat. The books consisted of fifty-two thousand volumes, mainly religious, but some were tales of foreign travel, and there were schoolbooks for their children.

7. Farming and Smuggling

Norfolk has always been primarily an agricultural county, and for several centuries there was a relationship between farming and smuggling. Sheep-farming provided wool, the most profitable commodity to smuggle in medieval times, and later the Tudor Corn Laws, which prohibited the export of corn, caused grain to be smuggled abroad. Farmers did not hesitate to smuggle goods when it suited them, as it did in the 1540s when the French ports of Calais and Boulogne were occupied by the English and His Majesty's provisioners were responsible for supplying the garrisons. Large quantities of butter and cheese were required, much of which was provided by Norfolk and Suffolk farmers. However, it would appear that they found it more profitable to sell their produce locally and so smuggled it into Norwich, Ipswich and Colchester after dark. Letters were sent by the Privy Council in 1545 to the Mayor of Norwich, and bailiffs of the other towns, informing them of this practice and pointing out that the 'Kings Magestes provisioners were greatly defrauded and empeched of the provision of Calays and Bulloigne'. They were instructed by the Council to allow the bearers of the letters to carry out house-to-house searches for butter and cheese, and to see what stocks they could find before reporting back to the Council for instructions. No doubt the farmers of Norfolk and Suffolk were not too upset when they heard that these ports had been lost to the French in 1558.

By the last decade of the seventeenth century, the smuggling industry had undergone several major changes. First, import smuggling had superseded export smuggling, and geneva and tea were the main commodities being smuggled from the continent into Britain. Second, smuggling had become labour-intensive, and large numbers of men, horses and carts, were needed to transport contraband from the coasts. Farms were able to supply much of the transport and men, and many farmers and farm labourers found smuggling a lucrative occupation; farm work often took second place to smuggling. Sometimes farmers smuggled goods on their own account, or had shares in a cargo, but they were mainly responsible for providing the bulk of the transport for getting contraband away from the beaches to destinations inland, by lending their horses and vehicles for that purpose.

As time passed, many farmers found that smuggling had its disadvantages, especially at harvest time when additional labour was required to bring in the harvest. It was reported in the *Gentleman's Magazine*, 1734, that the daily wage of a labourer was 18d., but the farmers of Suffolk found it difficult to get labourers to work for them. The reason for this was that the smugglers paid them 2s. 6d. a day to wait at the coast for the landing of goods. As soon as the goods were landed, the men mounted on horseback would take them inland and dispose of them. Whilst transporting the goods they were paid a guinea a day and were well entertained during their attendance.

Just how well the smugglers were entertained was shown in June 1733, when a party of twenty-five smugglers arrived at a farmhouse in Shelton, twelve miles south of Norwich, in the middle of the night. They knocked at the doors until the farmer and some of his servants came out, then demanded to know what victuals were in the house. They were told that, among other things, there was pork and beef. However these things did not appeal to them. The farmer told them he was going to kill a calf the following day, but if they wished he would kill it and they could have part of it. The smugglers agreed, the calf was killed and a quarter of it dressed for them. Later, having eaten their fill, the smugglers gave the farmer five guineas plus five shillings each to the servants attending, and went on their way.

It was reported in the *Gentleman's Magazine* that smugglers went about in gangs of forty to fifty men and might soon be a danger to civil government, as they were so well mounted that not even the dragoons could stop them. However, sometimes members of these gangs were arrested by customs officers, as in March 1784, when two men from a gang, consisting of Suffolk and Norfolk men, were committed to Ipswich Gaol. One, William Denny Fox, was a wealthy farmer from Benacre in Suffolk, and the other was Samuel Custin of Great Yarmouth. They were charged with carrying firearms and other offensive weapons, and aiding and assisting in running contraband goods.

It was not surprising that farmers were looked upon with suspicion by customs and excise officers. This was the case in 1792 when a Deopham farmer wrote to the *Norwich Mercury* complaining about the behaviour of some excise officers. He complained of the unjustified treatment he had experienced when four excise officers, some armed, entered his house under the pretence of searching for smuggled goods. The officers had obtained a warrant on information supplied by an informer. When he assured them that they had been misinformed and demanded to know by what authority they had presumed to take such a step, they 'grossly insulted him'. The correspondent said that his motive in mentioning this incident was to show that magistrates needed to be more cautious and better advised upon the grounds for applying for a warrant, before it was granted. 'As it could not be the intention of Government that His Majesty's peaceable subjects should be exposed to the insolence and outrage of his servants'.

Another Norfolk farmer, when he was fined £36 for smuggling, claimed that it was his fear of a gang of smugglers that caused him to act unwisely. In 1774, William Fawsset had a farm at North Wootton, just north of King's Lynn, which extended down to the banks of the Great Ouse. In a petition to the Commissioners of Excise he stated that his shepherd had informed him that his labourers had found some liquor in a crop of wheat on his land. When he went to the field, he found three of his men lying near the gate with an empty cask, which they said had contained gin. He asked them what they had found, and one of the men went into the field and returned with three half-ankers. His men told him there were more casks hidden in his wheat, and in the adjoining crop of beans. Fawsset maintained that he did not see any other casks, but told his men to carry the three they had to his house. He swore that he did not sample the contents or know what they contained. He did not want them for his own use, nor did he realise that he had committed an offence by taking them to his own house, claiming that he was ignorant of the laws relating to revenue, and had decided to seek advice on what he should do with the casks.

The following day he went to an attorney for advice on how to act in this matter and was told to inform an officer of excise. However, when he returned home his wife told him that a man had been enquiring about the liquor and wished to speak to him and would be waiting for him in the little alehouse in the parish. When he arrived at the alehouse, he was told by the landlord and his wife that they had overheard the smugglers saying that if they did not get their liquor back, they would set fire to every house in the village. Fawsset said that he was frightened that the smugglers would set fire to his house and barn if he did not give it to them. That evening a man came to his door and demanded the casks, which he gave him, as he dared not refuse. The man, with the help of others, then removed the other casks, which his labourers had told him were in the wheat and beans. Fawsset also stated that he could not understand why he had been fined £36 as half-ankers contained five gallons each and their full value was not above 7s. per gallon. He thought the heaviest penalty he could incur by the law was treble the value of the goods and he could not understand therefore why he had to pay the full penalty of £36.

However, some smuggling farmers not only took an active part in running contraband, but were prepared to use violence when their goods were seized. In July 1784, a farmer and two other smugglers were arrested at Thornham on the north Norfolk coast. Their houses were surrounded by a party of Elliot's light horse and they were immediately taken to Lynn. They were put in post chaises, conducted under escort to London and committed to Newgate Prison. They were charged with rescuing a large quantity of goods which had been seized, and 'cruelly treating the officers'. The speed at which they were removed from the area gave their smuggling associates no chance to get together and attempt to rescue them. Smugglers in that neighbourhood had been known to attack and disarm revenue officers and soldiers.

Shepherds and their flocks were also made use of by smugglers on the Norfolk coast. Where there were no harbours, as at Heacham and Hunstanton, coal vessels and other small craft unloaded their cargoes on the beaches. In the spreading sandy flats on this coast, the tracks of wild birds, animals and people can be easily distinguished. The main problem for the smugglers of one hundred and fifty years ago was how to cover the tracks they left in their passage across to the hard roads.

For the usual consideration (a keg of the 'right stuff'), the local shepherds usually solved this problem for them by driving their flocks along the sandy trail left by a gang of smugglers, completely obliterating all evidence that contraband goods had passed that way.

Farms provided many hiding places for contraband, some of a temporary nature, for example among growing crops, especially corn. In August 1775, some excise officers discovered 70 half-ankers of foreign brandy and geneva, which they seized in a cornfield at Ellingham. Other places used for concealing smuggled goods were woodland, marl-pits or under freshly-turned soil. Barns were often used but they were risky places, as they were certain to be searched if the farmer was suspected of being involved in smuggling. Some farmers therefore went to great lengths to construct more permanent hiding places, such as those at Gimingham, about two miles inland from the north-east coast, where the lawn at Rookery Farm was said to cover secret hiding places for smuggled goods.

An interesting story was told at the turn of the century by an old lady who in her childhood in the 1820s stayed in a farmhouse about three miles from the sea. One night during her stay, she heard rumbling carts and men whispering beneath her bedroom window. The following morning she enquired about what she had heard, and was told that it was normal farm work being carried out. She accepted this explanation until a party of preventive men arrived and searched the farm, having followed the tracks from a cliff-top gap to the farmhouse. There was little doubt that contraband was on the premises, but a thorough search revealed nothing and the preventive men eventually left. There was one place they had not looked, however, and that was beneath the sawdust in a sawpit, where there was a cunningly-devised store house.

From the sixteenth century to the early years of the nineteenth century important changes in agriculture and land use took place. During this time open field strip farming was gradually replaced by more consolidated farms, with enclosed fields, many of which were taken from common and heathland. In the latter half of the eighteenth century, many Norfolk parishes had still not been enclosed and the following seizures of contraband were reported in the *Norwich Mercury*. In February 1777, two riding officers, assisted by some dragoons, seized 70 half-ankers of brandy and geneva in Hempstead Field, and in November that year Mr Colby, a riding officer at Caister, seized 400 lbs of tea and 3½ ankers of geneva in Filby Field. The following month the same officer, accompanied by six excise officers and three dragoons, intercepted about thirty smugglers in Billockby Field and during the skirmish one of the officers and a soldier were slightly wounded, and a smuggler's horse was shot. The officers and soldiers seized 3,300 lbs. of tea and 113 half-ankers of geneva. Four years later in November 1781, an excise officer from

Foulsham seized 19 half-ankers of brandy, 11 half-ankers of geneva and 180 lbs. of tea in Bawdeswell Field.

How did the changes in agriculture affect smuggling in Norfolk? It was the enclosure of common and heathland that was to have an effect on smuggling. Before these lands were enclosed and cultivated, they consisted of large open areas of heather, bracken, gorse, trees, wild plants and shrubs. They were often uneven, with ridges and hollows. Although the main roads did cross them, it was the numerous narrow trackways that gave good cover to the smugglers' packhorses, especially after dark.

The pathway across Cawston Heath, scene of an incident in 1771.

One night in July 1771, when a King's Officer was crossing Cawston Heath, between 11 o'clock and midnight, he met five mounted smugglers. Two of their horses were loaded with 8 half-ankers of brandy and the other three with tea. He followed them for six miles, but met nobody who could assist him, so he only managed to seize 2 half-ankers and the smugglers went on with the rest of their goods unmolested.

Common and heathland also provided good temporary hiding places for contraband, and reports of seizures made by the revenue officers confirm this. In April 1768, two riding officers seized 54 half-ankers of geneva on Witton Heath near North Walsham and in February 1783 a party of customs and excise officers, with a number of dragoons quartered at Holt, seized 12¼cwt. of tea among the furze on Runton Heath near Cromer. Other reports mention Mousehold Heath on the outskirts of Norwich which was very useful to smugglers who wished to hide their goods until it was safe to take them into the city. In July 1791, some Norwich excise

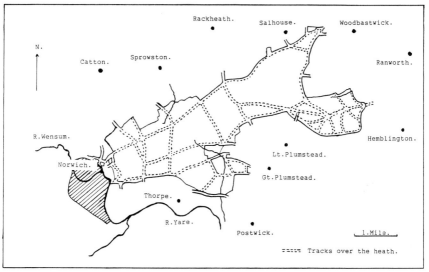

Mousehold Heath in the late eighteenth century.
This heath was regularly used by smugglers.

officers seized 312 gallons of foreign spirits, 78 lbs. of tea and 1,100 lbs. of tobacco. The following February 12 gallons of foreign brandy, 40 gallons of geneva, 7 lbs. of tea and 150 lbs. of tobacco were also seized on the heath.

By the early years of the nineteenth century, most of Norfolk's commons and heathlands had been enclosed and were under cultivation. At one time Mousehold Heath extended up to six miles from the city boundary, almost to the edge of the Broads, and was about two miles in width at its widest point. Today less than two hundred acres remain. Thirteen hundred acres of Cawston Heath were enclosed in 1801 and only a small part of the heath can be seen today. Arthur Young, writing in 1804, underlined the value of these lands to smugglers and others, when he stated that one thousand acres of Hevingham Common, enclosed in 1799, had been 'the source of all sorts of immorality, poaching, smuggling, etc.'. With the enclosure of these lands the smugglers lost many of their best hiding places and were forced to use the roads more. This increased the possibility of their capture.

In *The Vale of Health or Overstrand and Sidestrand Past and Present*, published in 1899, George Beckett recorded that local farmers willingly helped smugglers to transport their goods. Their horses and carts were frequently used to convey a cargo to some inland destination. On dark, cloudy nights the loaded carts travelled with muffled harness; no driver's whip cracked as the well-trained horses responded to a whisper. The following morning they would return empty. Farmers would leave their best teams at the smugglers' disposal and it was not uncommon in those days for the farmer's horses to be suddenly harnessed up during the night without permission, but it was customary on returning the horses to the stable for the smugglers to leave a substantial present for the farmer.

An old man, who had died before 1899, had worked on a local farm as a boy. One of his duties was to collect the cattle from the fields and drive them to some isolated farm buildings, which had no house attached to them. One night in winter, when darkness came on suddenly, he collected the cattle from the fields as usual and drove them to the outbuildings. When he entered the buildings he was surprised to find a man in one of them in charge of four horses, fully equipped to go on a journey. Before he left he was cautioned by the man who told him to 'know nothing' about what he had seen. When he returned the following morning to collect the cattle he found that both the man and the horses had gone.

The Reverend W. H. Marcon became Rector of Edgefield in 1876. In his *Reminiscences of a Norfolk Parson*, published in 1927, he recorded several stories he had heard when his elderly parishioners discussed old times together. A man once said that he had to go down to Blakeney Quay to get a cart of liquor. All the horses and carts rattled down on the quay where the tubs stood. There were hundreds of them and they were all loaded on the carts and away within a quarter of an hour. As soon as they were out of the town, they heard the guns of the preventive men being fired behind them. They never hit anybody because it had all been planned; they knew where to find some tubs that had been left for them, but they kept on firing after the carts had gone, so that people would think that they had almost caught them. He said that they were paid half a crown a night and sometimes they would have to go ten nights before a ship came in, then they would get five shillings apiece. They always left a tub inside the Parson's gate. 'Why in this house where we are sitting,' he said 'I

Blakeney Quay.
Large quantities of smuggled spirits were often landed
here after dark.

have seen the chamber right cram full o' casks, so that they had to prop up the ceiling with larch poles'.

The speaker then told the following story about when the preventive men were eventually replaced by coastguards, men drawn from the Navy, who were stricter where duty was concerned. One night all the carts and horses were seized by the coastguards and stalled at Weybourne ready to be sold by auction. The owners went to the narrator's farmer friend and said 'Look here sir, they won't suspect you. Do you go down to Weybourne and see what you can do'. The farmer went to Weybourne and found the horses in the charge of a sailor who knew no more about horses than a cow knew about the gable end of a barn. Moreover it was in July, a time when horses shed their coats. The farmer asked to look at the horses. He then went up to the first horse's tail and pulled a handful of hair out of its haunches and exclaimed, 'Here's a rare bad job here! Do you know what this horse has got? He's got the mange! See what I have pulled out. I shouldn't wonder but what they've all got it, that's a wonderful catching thing'. He then went down to the stable and pulled a handful of hair out of each horse. The sailor did not know

117

what to do with the horses, and the farmer said that it was no use putting them up for sale as nobody would buy them for fear of giving it to their own horses. The farmer then offered the sailor £5 for the lot. The bargain was closed and that night every horse was back in its own stable.

The Reverend Marcon asked what became of all the contraband. The man replied that it used to go to different places, some long way off. 'I have known my father drive a tamer for old Mr ... and go with a wagon full o' thorns into Suffolk and be gone for a week at a time. That was only thorns on top, for you've a nigh guess that they've enough thorns of their own in Suffolk, but in the boke of the wagon was bacca and liquor.'

A correspondent writing in the *Eastern Daily Press* in January 1931 related the following story he had been told as a boy. One night some smugglers were transporting contraband in a cart pulled by an old black mare, when they were surprised by excise officers. The smugglers escaped but the cart and goods were seized. Not surprisingly nobody claimed the mare, so she was advertised for sale by auction. She was kept in a field behind Cromer Coastguard Station and the night before the auction was to take place she disappeared. The excise officers searched several farms they suspected might have had something to do with her removal from the field, but could find no trace of her. What had happened was that her owner had gone to the field and called her to him. He then put a halter on her and quietly led her home. On arrival he carefully poured two pails of whitewash over her, which he had previously prepared. The following day the excise officers paid him a visit and searched his farm for the black mare; they never thought to give the grey mare feeding at the far end of the field a second glance and left empty-handed. Another source named the farmer involved as Mr Playford of Northrepps.

Apart from losing their horses and carts, the men who went down to the coast to collect smuggled goods risked being wounded or even killed if there was a confrontation with preventive men, or later the coastguard. One night in December 1826, a lieutenant in the Preventive Service stationed at Cromer tackled a gang of smugglers single-handed. He was just retiring to bed when he received information that several carts were below the cliffs just north of the town ready to take a cargo of contraband, and if he waited at a certain place, it would not be long before they passed. He went to the place alone, and waited for the arrival of the carts. Soon seven carts appeared and the officer grabbed the head of the first horse, shouted who he was, and ordered them to stop. One of the gang made use of 'some coarse language' and threatened to murder him. The officer immediately drew his pistol and shot the man. His companions picked him up, put him in an empty cart and quickly drove off. The officer then searched all the carts which he found to be empty.

Some Norfolk farmers who smuggled goods for many years became very wealthy. Mark Butcher of Earsham was a farmer and liquor merchant, and much of his wealth was thought to have been derived from smuggling. Butcher was born about 1734 and married Mary Benham in 1763 at All Saints Church, Earsham, where he became a churchwarden. He was already known for his smuggling locally and when he had a tomb built on the north side of the church, about nine yards from the church wall, his motives for doing so were suspected by some people. The Reverend G. Sandby sent a letter, dated 1771, to the Norwich Archdeaconry Court, in which he described the tomb erected by Mark Butcher. He suggested that Butcher had gone above his station in building such a large tomb, and suspected that it would be used to store smuggled goods. Sandby asked for advice on how he should act in this matter. The Court replied that since Butcher had built the tomb without obtaining a licence from the Church authorities it should be demolished. Nevertheless Butcher got his way because the tomb was not demolished and can be seen in Earsham churchyard today.

In February 1783, Mark Butcher appeared before Mr Baron Eyre in the Exchequer Court, charged with running foreign geneva. He was charged on information supplied by several excise officers who had seized a large quantity of geneva in his warehouse. During the trial many witnesses were called for the Crown, including the excise officers, who had supplied the information. However they gave such 'contradictory and improbable evidence' that no credit was given to it. It was stated that the officers had seized British geneva on pretence that it was foreign and had been run by Butcher. Several important people in the liquor trade were also called by the Crown to give their opinion on the quality of the liquor that had been seized, and all gave evidence in favour of the defendant, except one, who was reputedly biased by prejudice and self-interest. After a long trial, Butcher was found not guilty before a crowded court.

Mark Butcher's tomb in All Saints' Churchyard, Earsham.
He built it many years before his death, possibly to store
contraband.

There was little doubt that this was a popular verdict, especially in Earsham and Bungay, where celebrations were held, which included illuminations, gun-firing and bell-ringing. Butcher may well have employed or supplied many of the people involved. However he was fortunate that smugglers had a great deal of public sympathy at this time. This sympathy was shown by the *Norfolk Chronicle,* in the last paragraph of its report on the trial, when it referred to the excise officers. 'The public shewed their detestation of the insolent and alarming proceedings of those engines of oppression, in their unlawful seizure of so large a portion of the property of an innocent individual, by the most extravagant demonstrations of joy on their discomfiture which was testified in Bungay, and Earsham, by illuminations, firing of guns, ringing of bells etc.'

Later in September that year, the *Norwich Mercury* expressed concern about smuggling, when it reported that it was well known that encouragement was given to these 'idle and disorderly persons by different ranks of people', which was 'astonishing and truly alarming'. The report referred to the acquittal of 'a very notorious smuggler' tried earlier in the year and to the celebrations in particular places on account of his acquittal. Although it did not name him, the report was obviously referring to Mark Butcher. However he was never convicted of smuggling and when he died in January 1809, aged seventy-five years, he was buried at Earsham in the tomb he had erected in All Saints churchyard. He had acquired great wealth and left his family well provided for. His eldest surviving son, Robert, inherited his farms and public houses in Norfolk and Suffolk and several other properties.

Some years later, in August 1829, when public sympathy no longer favoured the smugglers, Ireland Watts, who kept a small farm and The Barge public house at Antingham, appeared with his brother, Robert, before Norfolk Assizes, charged with obstructing customs officers in the course of their duty. Captain De Lafosse, the officer at Mundesley, traced contraband goods to the defendant's house at Antingham. He left to get assistance and returned later with Lieutenant Lee, several coastguards and a peace officer. They demanded to be admitted to the house, but the defendants refused to let them in. The Captain then drew his pistol and threatened to fire, but Robert Watts merely bared his chest and shouted 'Fire and be damned'. Captain De Lafosse, fearing he could not enter the house without bloodshed, withdrew his men.

Soon after the officer and his men had left the scene, a loaded cart was driven away from the house, and Robert Watts was heard instructing the driver to 'Flog 'em along!' Meanwhile the Captain had informed Watts' landlord, Lord Suffield, and he went to the house. When he arrived Lord Suffield confronted the Watts brothers saying, 'I put you into this house on the faith that you would leave off your old tricks'. The house was searched, but no contraband was found. In court the defence submitted that the Captain's authority did not permit him to search the house. However, the special jury returned a verdict of guilty. The brothers were later able to appeal against the verdict.

Just how much smuggling helped the poor by giving them an opportunity to earn extra money is not known, but Arthur Young in his *General View of the Agriculture of the County of Norfolk,* published in 1804, said that the living of the poor had considerably altered in his memory. They now lived better, except in the article of beer, which the high price of malt had stopped them brewing, driving them to the alehouses and gin shops. These observations by Young show why there was a constant demand for cheap gin, much of which may have been supplied by the smugglers.

As for the farmers, smuggling provided a good income, especially in the times of poor harvests. A book about north Norfolk farm work written in the nineteenth century, by Mrs Gerard Creswell, *Eighteen Years on the Sandringham Estate*, referred to one or two prosperous farmers of whom it was said 'they made their money in the smuggling times' or 'they broke up a rare smuggling lot on his place once upon a time, but he'd taken good care of himself afore it was found out!'.

It was once reported that many farmers in north Norfolk had shares in smuggled cargoes and if they were landed successfully they would reap a 100% profit, which fully repaid them for the loan of their horses and carts. The economic links between smuggling and farming were vital to some farmers. In an article written in the *Eastern Daily Press*, December 29th 1930, by D. H. Parry, entitled 'A Smuggling Memory', he wrote of a friend of his who was in conversation with a farmer whose family had tilled the soil for many generations on the Norfolk coast. His friend had said,

'You farmers are always grumbling. How comes it that if things were so bad your people have stuck to the land all these centuries and made money?'

'Because they made it out of smuggling,' the farmer replied.

8. Public Attitudes to the Free Traders

People's attitudes to the free traders varied considerably. At one end of the scale were those honest traders whose businesses were threatened, and, at the other, those who did not see smuggling as a crime and regularly purchased smuggled goods. Apart from the honest traders in tea and spirits in the 1780s there were the merchants, wool dealers and industrialists in the county, and particularly those in Norwich, who campaigned against wool smuggling. The concern of these men and their efforts to suppress smuggling were widely reported in the local newspapers, but the silent majority of the people either kept on smuggling, or continued to purchase contraband.

There were virtually no reports of wool smuggling in Norfolk in the local newspapers in the second half of the eighteenth century. Although wool smuggling appears to have been minimal in the county, it was still being carried on extensively in many other parts of the country. This was shown when 7,845 lbs. of condemned wool were put on sale at Rye Custom House, in Sussex, on Thursday 19th December 1782. This was of particular concern to the manufacturers, merchants and wool dealers, many of whom carried on their trades in Norfolk.

In June 1786, a wool meeting was held in London at the Crown and Anchor tavern in the Strand. It was well attended by merchants, manufacturers and wool dealers from all over the country, including a number from Norfolk. The chairman read a letter concerning smuggling from Penrhyn, on the Welsh coast. It reported that a large party of smugglers armed with firearms was discovered by customs officers in the act of loading a considerable quantity of worsted yarn, about 2,000 lbs., on board a vessel lying off that coast. A fierce battle took place between the officers and the smugglers, which resulted in one of the officers being seriously wounded. The officers managed to seize about 240 lbs. of yarn, but the remainder was put on board the vessel by the smugglers.

Since large quantities of worsted cloth were being produced in Norfolk at this time, this news was of particular concern to the county's industrialists present. It was agreed that a Bill should be put through Parliament 'for the more effectual prevention of the practice of wool smuggling'. The local M.P.s, Sir H. Harbord and Mr Windham, were present at the meeting and promised to give the Bill their support.

Nothing seems to have been done until two years later, when in April a committee of merchants met in London, at the Crown and Anchor, to discuss a Wool Bill. There had been a significant drop in the woollen orders from Spain and many correspondents attributed this largely to the wool smuggling to France, which enabled the French to undersell in foreign markets. Others admitted that smuggling did go on, but thought it had not increased and was therefore not responsible for the decrease in orders. In June that year, the Wool Bill was debated in the House of Lords. The Norwich representative, Alderman Ives, told the Lords that the declining state of trade was due to heavy duties levied on fabrics in foreign countries, the fashion of wearing linens in preference to stuffs, and the smuggling of wool.

Two years later the Norwich manufacturers were still concerned about wool smuggling. When they met in December 1790, they were informed of a seizure of wool, intended to have been exported to France, made by a Captain Sharp of Dover. It appeared that a person had been exporting raw wool from Dover in parcels weighing only a stone for three years. According to the *Norwich Mercury,* steps were being taken 'to support the prosecution of this delinquent'.

At this time another voice was heard condemning smuggling. It was that of the founder of the Methodist movement, John Wesley, who was very much against smuggling and referred to the trade as 'the accursed thing'. He published a pamphlet saying that smugglers were thieves who picked the pockets of the King and his subjects. While he was on his preaching tours throughout the country, he regularly attacked smuggling and to show his dislike for the trade, he refused to drink tea. Few people involved with smuggling took any notice of his words, and he realised that his labours on the subject were in vain.

Many Church of England parsons were happy to assist, or deal with the smugglers. The best-known in Norfolk was the diarist and Rector of Weston Longville, 1776-1803, Parson Woodforde. He received a regular supply of spirits and other goods from the local smugglers, and often recorded his purchases in his diary. One entry in

January 1777 stated that Richard Andrews, a smuggler, had brought him a pound of tea, for which he paid 9s., and three silk Indian handkerchiefs, for which he paid 5s.6d. each. He regularly paid 25s. for a four-gallon tub of gin supplied by the smugglers, and usually tipped the men who brought it a shilling for their trouble. On November 26th 1786, he recorded that Clerk Hewitt of Mattishall Burgh delivered a tub of gin while he was at dinner and stayed to dine with his staff in the kitchen. Woodforde usually bottled his gin and once, when a tub was short by two or three bottles, the smugglers allowed him three shillings off his next tub.

**Revd James Woodforde
Rector of Weston Longville,
a regular customer of the
smugglers.**

Sometimes he did not see the smugglers when they came. On December 29th 1786, he heard a thump at his front door about nine o'clock in the evening, and when he went to investigate he found two tubs, one of gin and the other of cognac, but nobody was there.

On September 15th 1792, Woodforde had a tub of rum delivered in the evening. Soon after he heard that John Buck, the blacksmith at Honingham, had been informed against, and a tub of smuggled gin was found in his house by two excise officers. He got up very early on the morning of the 17th to hide his smuggled rum, probably to bury it. He knew that he could be fined £10 for purchasing smuggled goods, and that Buck, the seller, could be fined £50, but if he chose to inform against his customers, he could be pardoned his own offence. Woodforde need not have worried as the blacksmith got off with a light fine and did not inform against anyone.

Peter Forster, the flour merchant and miller at Lenwade Bridge, sold Woodforde flour and ground his corn for him. The Forsters were successful business people and, like the parson, were prepared to purchase goods from the smugglers. A copper coalscuttle, which was used to house smuggled tea, was passed down for several generations in this family.

The Watermill at Lenwade Bridge.
Peter Forster, the miller in the late eighteenth century bought tea from
the smugglers and kept it in a copper coalscuttle.

When the Reverend Henry Ready took over the living of
Waxham-cum-Palling, on the east coast of Norfolk, in the first half of
the nineteenth century, the Reverend John Cubitt, his predecessor
who held the living for many years, advised him always to open the
front door of the Rectory at daybreak. If there was a tub of brandy on
the doorstep, he was to take it in and not to allow anyone to enter his
barn for several days, as it was being used by smugglers. To indicate
that the barn was clear again, the smugglers would leave another tub
by way of rent.

This part of the coast was regularly used by smugglers landing
goods that, once clear of the beach, could be easily and safely
distributed all over the county along the rivers and broads. The main
risk was getting the contraband across the beach and over three miles
of marshes. The parson's barn, being above suspicion, was con-
veniently near Hickling Broad and therefore frequently used by the
smugglers.

Years later the Reverend Ready would recall 'those good old

days', which he said came to an end when telegraphic communication between England and the continent was established. As soon as a cargo of brandy, silk, cigars etc. had left a French port, informers would telegraph its destination to the English Custom House and the smugglers were usually caught and their goods confiscated.

Smuggled goods were sometimes sold by public auction on market days in the county towns. Occasionally members of the public were hostile towards the officers supervising these sales. In February 1805, a riot broke out at North Walsham when James Mackarel, an excise officer, was conducting one of these sales. Mackarel had seized a quantity of smuggled spirits that had been condemned and ordered to be sold by public auction on a market day. A crowd assembled and began jostling the officer so roughly that he injured his ankles and was lame for several weeks. Five men eventually appeared before the Norfolk Assizes charged with assaulting the officer in the execution of his duty. These men were all acquitted except one, John Wake, who later appeared before the Court of King's Bench. In his defence Wake stated that he was selling wheat in the market place, when a great mob suddenly arose and carried him into the place of sale. He claimed he was unable to extricate himself from the crowd and had no intention of interrupting the officer as he was himself one of the surveyors of taxes for the county. An affidavit from the clerk of the corn market confirmed this statement, and several others from Horatio Lord Walpole, Charles Windham Esq., Sir Roger Kerrison Baronet, of Norwich, and four other gentlemen in the county were read concerning the defendant's good character. He was ordered to stand committed to Newgate and to be brought before the court again at a later date. Nothing further seems to have been reported about this case.

In the early years of the nineteenth century, the attitude of the courts had changed considerably towards the smugglers and others who defrauded the Revenue. This was shown in 1813 when a conspiracy between two Norwich excise officers and a maltster came to light. Shylock Parsons, an excise officer, and Manning, a supervisor, had made false returns of the duty due from one J. Potter, a maltster, for malt which he had made wet. These officers, including one who had since turned informer, had been in the habit of tearing leaves out of the excise book which had the duties properly entered and 'interleaving others, with much less duty inserted'.

Potter and Parsons appeared before the Court of King's Bench in November, when they were charged with these offences; Manning had previously absconded. They were found guilty, but before he pronounced their sentences Mr Justice Le Blanc remarked that the conspiracy to defraud the Revenue as detailed in this case was as wicked as he had ever known. He stated that some people were in the habit of thinking more lightly of frauds against the Revenue than of other frauds. He pointed out that not only was the Revenue injured, but also *every* fair trader by the unfair advantage the smuggler gained by his fraudulent practices. The offenders were each sentenced to one year's imprisonment in Norwich Gaol, and to stand in the pillory. Potter was also to serve an additional three months after being found guilty of a similar offence.

Many Norfolk people were ready to sample free smuggled spirits if they came their way. It was necessary for smugglers, therefore, when hiding their goods from the revenue officers and watchmen in the towns, to ensure they were not observed by members of the general public. Some people would not hesitate to take any contraband goods they discovered either for their own use, or to the revenue officers in the hope of receiving a share in any reward. In November 1773, a Norwich weaver saw a smuggler unloading several half-ankers of gin and putting them in a cowshed at Magdalen Gates. When the smuggler had left, the weaver told several other people and they went to the cowshed where they found 11 half-ankers of gin. They took the gin and drank as much as they wanted and then sold what was left to their neighbours at a 'reasonable cost'.

After making a seizure both customs and excise officers had to be careful when they allowed members of the public to help them remove the contraband from the scene to their warehouses. In some cases the people assisting the officers were the smugglers themselves, looking for an opportunity to get their goods back.

However, to some members of the public, contraband was fair game if they could get their hands on it. Whether it was a cache hidden by the smugglers or a quantity of smuggled goods already seized by the revenue officers did not matter to them. In January 1764, the customs officers at Cromer, assisted by some local men, seized a large quantity of geneva from a smuggling vessel. They carried the liquor ashore and put it in a house near the sea. That night the house was broken into, a hole was made in one of the walls, and 26 double-stoup bottles of liquor were taken. The following day a thorough search was made of the town and all the bottles were found in the possession of three men, Henry Paine, John Paine, his son, and John Rook, their cousin. John Paine and John Rook had assisted the officers with the original seizure and the three of them were taken before a magistrate who committed them to Norwich Castle.

People seem to have drunk excessively when they had access to a quantity of contraband liquor, and it was not unusual for them to drink themselves to death under such circumstances. This may partly be explained by the fact that to save tubs the smugglers sometimes shipped their spirits greatly over proof and diluted them on their arrival in this country. Some smuggled spirits were as much as 180% over proof when they were landed. (See Glossary)

From time to time there were reports in the Norfolk newspapers of people dying after drinking smuggled spirits. On Sunday February 12th 1768, some excise officers with a party of invalids, men from the services no longer fit for active service, were passing through Fritton on their way to Yarmouth when they discovered 56 half-ankers of liquor concealed among some alder trees. They seized them and conveyed them to Yarmouth Excise Office. It was later discovered that one of the invalids was missing and a search was made for him. On the following Tuesday he was found dead by his comrades, some distance from the town. It was thought that he had made too free with some of the liquor and had eventually died from exposure.

It was customary for customs and excise officers to reward people who assisted them when they made a seizure of spirits by giving them a tub. On Tuesday October 12th 1773, a seizure of 36 half-ankers of gin was made on the beach at Cley, and six women who assisted the officers were given one. Between them they consumed 18 pints and lapsed into an alcoholic stupor. Four of them recovered the next day but the other two were still speechless on the following Thursday, and their recovery was thought doubtful.

An incident was reported one night in October 1786, when a French smuggling lugger was seized and taken into Blakeney Harbour. There were 240 half-ankers of spirits on board, and before these could be conveyed to the Custom House, several local people boarded the lugger. They helped themselves to the spirits and drank so heavily that two of them fell overboard and were drowned. In April 1801, a large number of tubs containing foreign spirits were seen floating in the sea off Happisburgh. A number of labouring men managed to draw some ashore and stave them. These men then drank to such excess that one of them died the following day and two others almost lost their lives.

It was reported in the *Norwich Mercury* that a man had died through excessive drinking on Sunday December 8th 1823. Two brothers named Burton, belonging to the parish of Sedgeford, thirteen miles north-east of King's Lynn, were passing through Burnham Market, when the congregation was assembling at the church for the evening service at 3 o'clock. Both men were 'in a disgraceful state of intoxication', and one of the Burnham constables was ordered to take them into custody and put them in temporary confinement. After the evening service, when the constable went to release the brothers, he found one of them dead. The survivor said that they had been drinking spirits but he would not say where they had obtained them.

An inquest was held at the Hoste Arms, Burnham Market, on David Burton. A witness said that he had seen the deceased and his brother at the house of Mr Ellis, a publican in Burnham Sutton, at twelve o'clock. After drinking two pints of beer and a small glass of gin between them, the brothers left. No account was given of their movements between twelve and three o'clock. It is possible that the Burton brothers found a cache of spirits hidden by some smugglers and drank excessively, a common occurrence in such cases. Since there were no reports of spirits being stolen and the surviving brother refused to say where they got them, possibly to avoid reprisals from the smugglers, this seems the most likely explanation.

Some smugglers did not think of themselves as criminals, as was shown in October 1769, when a man knocked on the door of Mr Bracey Taylor, a Yarmouth attorney. When the maid opened the door, he asked to speak to Mr Taylor and was shown to his office. He entered with a piece of black cloth over his face and demanded twenty guineas from Mr Taylor. He appeared to excuse himself for the robbery by telling his victim that he was a smuggler in great need of money and later, when he was able, he would see that Mr Taylor was repaid. However, when the attorney hesitated to comply with his wishes, the man struck him three times. Mr Taylor could only pay him five guineas, which was all he had in his office, and the man took them and left.

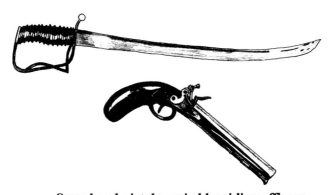

Sword and pistol carried by riding officers.
Re-drawn from *Smuggling, A History* by David Phillipson

Occasionally some people were public-spirited enough to go to the aid of the revenue officers when they attempted to seize contraband from the smugglers. An incident took place on a road near Norwich in February 1778, when an excise officer and a dragoon stopped a carrier's cart and seized several stoup bottles of geneva. The carrier, in an attempt to rescue the liquor, attacked and badly beat the officer and soldier. Luckily for them, a man went to their assistance and between them they almost beat the smuggler to death.

As the century progressed, it gradually became more difficult for the smugglers to keep their customers supplied with cheap spirits. The improvement in the Revenue services on land and at sea made it more hazardous for those running goods into the country. However some Norfolk people decided to make their own spirits. This, of course, was illegal and several people were prosecuted when their stills were discovered. In March 1824, the supervisor and excise officers at East Dereham, seized in the possession of one Robert Phillipo of Themelthorpe, 'a private still, cistern, several gallons of raw spirits, 4 bottles of geneva and 3 pieces of malt, one of which was drying on a kiln the others were in a state of vegetation.'

Some nine years later another private still was seized in a house in St Faith's Lane, Norwich. Fifteen gallons of spirits, recently worked, were also taken. The owners of the still were fined £30 and in default of payment were sentenced to three months' imprisonment.

Early in February 1844, three persons named Phillips, of Swanton Abbot, appeared before Lord Abinger and a special jury in the Court of Exchequer. They were accused of violating the excise laws by means of illicit distillation. The jury returned a verdict of guilty. The defendants had rendered themselves liable to penalties amounting to £12,000 but the Crown 'would be satisfied with a verdict for one penalty of £200, which trebled amounted to £600. Judgment was then entered for the last named sum.'

The attitude of the public towards smuggling was very important. While the public favoured the smugglers, the trade flourished in spite of strong opposition from some people. It was the industrialists and merchants whose businesses were threatened that were strongly opposed to smuggling. Towards the end of the eighteenth century, they pressed the Government for better laws against the smugglers. Their views were well publicised in the local press and their attitude towards smuggling, which many of them saw as a crime equal to poaching or highway robbery, was decidedly hostile.

However, the smugglers had the support of the majority of the population at this time, most of whom belonged to the labouring classes, who could not air their views in the press and had no influence in Parliament. Of course the better-off smugglers and their wealthier customers also kept quiet about their activities. Many of these people sat on juries in the courts when smugglers were tried and it was very difficult for prosecutors to get smugglers convicted, even when their guilt was obvious. In fact some Norfolk smugglers literally got away with murder. This was shown in the cases of Kemble and Gee previously mentioned. (See pages 57 and 77)

Generally there was little to discourage smugglers in the late eighteenth century and they took full advantage of these circumstances. The Government was not prepared to pay the revenue officers a reasonable salary and this led to many of them being tempted into collusion with the smugglers. Although many people favoured the smugglers, it did not stop them helping themselves whenever they came across unguarded contraband.

By the turn of the nineteenth century the situation had changed, and public sympathy for the smugglers had waned considerably. The courts were no longer lenient with the smugglers who appeared before them. This was shown in 1813, when the Court of King's Bench found Parsons, the excise officer, and Potter, the maltster, guilty of frauds against the Revenue and committed them to prison.

Many detained smugglers were confined in gaols or bridewells some distance from their home towns and villages. In November

1826, James Easy, described as 'a seafaring man from Dunwich in Suffolk', died in the Bridewell at Little Walsingham, in Norfolk, where he had been detained for over sixteen months as a Crown debtor for a smuggling transaction. He was sixty-four years old and the coroner's inquest decided his death was due to natural causes.

Three years earlier, on Sunday November 1st, an open boat was driven ashore on Sea Palling beach laden with spirits, 30 bales of tobacco and snuff and some paintings on wood. The boat and her cargo were seized by Thomas Williams and the preventive men of that station. The four smugglers on board were taken before a local magistrate, who ordered them to be detained at Wymondham Bridewell until they were due to appear before the Assize Court.

The former Bridewell, Little Walsingham.
In 1826 James Easy, a smuggler from Dunwich in Suffolk, died while confined here

By the second half of the nineteenth century, the public no longer looked favourably on the smuggler, but thought of him as a lawbreaker who cheated the honest traders. It was stated by John Bowring, an economist, that while the duties were high the smugglers were held in high esteem by the public, who saw them as benefactors, but with the coming of free trade the smugglers could no longer expect much sympathy from the British public.

9. Regional Smuggling

Smuggling took place throughout Norfolk, but as the landscape of the county varied considerably, it was easier to smuggle goods in some regions than in others. The fact that fewer reports were made of smuggling in some regions does not necessarily mean that little or no smuggling took place there. It could mean that those areas were difficult for the revenue officers to watch and that smugglers were able to transport their goods with less chance of them being seized. There was extensive smuggling along the whole length of the Norfolk coastline in the eighteenth and early nineteenth centuries. In his *Tour Through the Eastern Counties,* published in 1724, Daniel Defoe referred to his visit to the north Norfolk coast. He pointed out that the clandestine trade, or art, of smuggling was widely carried on in that area between England and Holland. Behind the wide flats of the north-west Norfolk salt marshes lie several silted-up and mostly deserted harbours and ports, which flourished in the eighteenth century. Creeks wind in and out of the marshes, and wherever there is a creek a village can be found. Like most of the county's coastal towns and villages, these were formerly smugglers' resorts.

A small navigable creek ran through the marshes to a warehouse at Thornham, where small boats were able to unload coal and load cargoes of corn. In February 1783, some excise officers from Wells and a party of dragoons seized about 4 cwt. of tea, buried in the sand at Thornham. In September the following year, the *Norfolk Chronicle* reported that a customs officer residing at Wolferton, assisted by a party of dragoons, had seized in Wolferton Creek a large boat laden with 137 half-ankers of brandy and geneva, and 5 cwt. of tea in 21 bags. Where there were no harbours, such as at Heacham and Hunstanton, smuggling vessels could easily unload their goods on the beach.

Further eastward the coastline is made up of low cliffs or dunes, and access to the shore used to be gained by cart gaps where horses and carts once made their way on to the beach. Revenue officers usually kept a close watch on these gaps and often searched and found contraband in the innocent-looking farm carts loaded with seaweed for manure, builders' carts laden with flints, or other carts

Morston Creek and Saltmarshes.
Typical scenery on the north Norfolk coast where smugglers landed their cargoes.

carrying fish, coal and other goods taken from boats pulled up on the beach. However, the smugglers, using mainly farm carts they had 'hired', made good use of these gaps under cover of darkness. It was between Sheringham and Weybourne that larger vessels could anchor nearer the shore than almost anywhere else on the Norfolk coast. In December 1823, the crew of the Sheringham preventive boat seized 87 half-ankers of geneva and a cask of tobacco on the beach at High Woman Gap, Runton. In the same month the crew of the Sheringham and Weybourne preventive boats seized 92 casks of geneva on Cley beach.

The sandy cliffs along the coast were constantly being washed away, so there were no convenient caves for the smugglers to hide their goods. In fact to hide contraband near the cliffs in some places could result in it being lost, as cliff-falls in the Cromer and Overstrand areas have been a common occurrence for centuries. In January 1825, there was a massive cliff-fall at Cromer when a 250 ft. high part, known as Lighthouse Hills, fell with great force on to the beach, extending itself beyond the waterline, some 300 yards, and covering about twelve acres of beach. The *Norwich Mercury*, January 25th, stated that it was fortunate that nobody was near it at the time, as officers and men of the Preventive Service were, in the course of their duty, obliged to pass in the night just where it fell.

Runton Gap.
This gap in the cliffs is typical of those on the north Norfolk coast that
gave access to the beach. They were frequently used by smugglers' carts
and packhorses when contraband was landed.

However, contraband could easily be buried on the sandy beaches
or among the wind-heaped dunes. This method of concealment was
favoured by many smugglers and large numbers of tubs were hidden
in this way on Norfolk beaches. It was reported in September 1774
that 150 half-ankers of gin and 14 bags of tea were found in a hole in
the sand, near the gallows on Yarmouth Denes. A drawback to this
method of concealment was that every now and then a storm or gale-
force wind would raise clouds of sand along the shore, and in a few
hours the contours of the sand dunes would be so changed that a
cache mound would be indistinguishable from a dozen others. It
sometimes happened that buried tubs were lost and only rediscovered
by accident many years later, when the wind and waves scoured away
the dunes and, as happened in the 1920s, the beach at Wells was
littered with rusty hoops and rotten staves. Further along, at Hemsby
on the east coast, a story is still told of how smugglers buried spirits in
the dunes and, when they returned to dig them up, could not find
them. It is not known whether they were removed secretly by some of

the smugglers, or whether their remains are still buried there today.

On Saturday April 24th 1779, at about 9.00 p.m., Christopher Cutting, the riding officer at Mundesley, with eight assistants, went to the Bacton Gap, where a boat belonging to a smuggling lugger was on the beach, and the crew were guarding a large quantity of uncustomed goods, which were buried in the sand. The smugglers had spent most of the night burying it, and were still working when the officer and his men arrived and promptly seized 65 half-ankers of brandy and some tea. However, before a wagon could be procured to carry them away, two smugglers on horseback rescued 7 bags of tea and called for assistance from the lugger anchored off the shore. The lugger immediately opened fire, while a dozen or more of her crew, armed with blunderbusses and pistols, manned one of her boats and rowed for the shore. When the boat reached the beach, her crew leapt out, drew their knives and threatened to rip Mr Cutting's 'belly open', which would have happened had they not been prevented by one of the mounted smugglers. The smugglers then loaded the goods back on board the lugger, except for 21 casks of geneva and 3 bags of tea.

If smugglers suspected they were being followed, or that their movements were being observed by revenue officers, or members of the public, they would soon punish the offenders. In August 1769, a gang of smugglers were going about their business near Happisburgh, when they noticed two men following them. They suspected that the men were spies, who were trying to find out where they hid their goods. The smugglers seized the men and tied them to a tree, poured liquor down their throats and left them. They remained like this for a considerable time before they were released by a passer-by.

One part of the north Norfolk coast on which the exploits of the smugglers have been well documented is that which includes the adjoining parishes of Northrepps, Overstrand, Sidestrand and Southrepps. The following are just two of the seizures reported in these parishes in the second half of the eighteenth century.

In December 1776, two revenue officers, John Jewell and Thomas Quincey, encountered a party of eight smugglers at Northrepps with a large quantity of foreign geneva and brandy in their possession. The officers managed to seize 20 half-ankers of geneva and 3 of brandy, but the smugglers escaped.

Overstrand beach was the scene of a seizure of contraband in March 1782 by Thomas Quincey, an excise officer, and William

Darby, a riding officer. After a long dispute with a number of smugglers the officers managed to take 33 half-ankers of geneva, which they took to the Excise Office at Holt.

In the mid-nineteenth century, Beckhythe, on the beach at Overstrand, was described as a fishing station consisting of a number of curing houses with four large and fourteen small fishing boats. The Norfolk newspapers reported several seizures there in the eighteenth century, the most notable being two made by the *Hunter* customs cutter just off the beach. In May 1787 she seized a cutter laden with 260 casks of foreign spirits and in July 1788 she captured a smuggling boat with a cargo of 105 casks of tobacco.

The smugglers in this area were just as prepared to defend their goods from revenue officers as they were anywhere else in the county. On the evening of Friday December 9th 1785, Thomas Scott, an Overstrand smuggler, was one of four men running a cargo of spirits. At about ten o'clock they were interrupted by William Darby. Scott violently attacked the officer but was eventually secured while the other three smugglers made their escape. He was detained until the following Monday, when he was taken before a magistrate who committed him to Norwich Castle. He was imprisoned there for about five years before being transferred to Newgate to await his trial at the Old Bailey, the verdict of which does not seem to have been reported locally.

One day in 1829, two ladies were watching ships from the cliffs at Northrepps, when they noticed a Yarmouth boat hovering off the shore. The ladies, Anna Gurney and Sarah Buxton, lived at Northrepps Cottage and the vessel may well have been observed by the preventive men who were ready for any run that might take place. That night a cargo was run at Overstrand and the ladies were woken by shouts and shots being fired in Shucks Lane near the entrance to their cottage. The preventive men had caught up with the smugglers who at first resisted but surrendered after two men had been killed.

One of the smugglers was Ted Summers, the Northrepps blacksmith, who managed to escape and was chased by the officers as far as his foundry. When he entered the foundry, one of the officers grabbed his coat, but he managed to shake him off and escape through the back door. Summers thought it expedient to retire for several weeks to one of his underground shelters, which he had made for just such an emergency, in Fox Hill Woods on Sir Samuel Hoare's

Shuck's Lane, Northrepps.
In 1829 two smugglers were killed here in a skirmish
with preventive men.

estate at Frogs' Hall. During his exile he would sometimes venture into Northrepps village disguised as an old woman. On one of his visits he was recognised by a child whose attempts to draw attention to him were quickly hushed by adults.

It was Summers who usually organised the smugglers in that neighbourhood when a run was to be made. Horses and carts were provided by the local people, particularly farmers. No doubt in some cases the horses were quite at ease obeying the commands of the smugglers at night, recognising the voices of the farm labourers they worked with during the day. Contraband was quickly transported into hiding places in the local plantations and buildings until it was safe to be moved inland. Ropes and pulleys were used to lift smuggled goods to the top of St Mary's church tower at Northrepps. Billy Silver, a local lad who worked in the gardens at Northrepps Hall, once drove a cart to Norwich on three successive nights. In his later years, Billy recalled his boyhood trips to Norwich. He said that he often drove a load of fish or even turnips to Norwich. He 'warnt' to go by the main road, but through Colby. He never helped with the loading and unloading and if asked he 'didn't know nuthen'.

It was not uncommon for whole villages to take part in smuggling and a further insight into the trade on the Norfolk coast was given by

Mr John Gray of Hungry Hill, Northrepps, who died in the early years of the twentieth century aged eighty-eight. He said the smugglers would watch for a boat to arrive off Beckhythe. When the cargo was to be run, both men and women went to help. He said that there was a vault in the garden of Church's Loke and another in the planting on Stone Hills. He had no chance to go smuggling himself, but his father, grandfather and grandmother did, and were well paid for the job. Most of the houses in the area took in barrels.

When Horace Walpole wrote of 'the wilds of Norfolk', in the eighteenth century, this description could easily have been applied to several large areas of the county, namely the salt marshes of the north Norfolk coast, Breckland in West Norfolk, and the many square miles of Broadland in the east of the county. It is thought that large quantities of contraband were transported along the waterways of Norfolk, for the most part unmolested by revenue officers. Broadland, with its rivers, broads and marshland supporting dense reed swamps, shrubs, alders and willows, provided numerous hiding places for contraband. Some broads were inaccessible on foot and could only be reached by boat. Such areas were difficult for revenue officers to search and this may account for so few seizures being reported there in the eighteenth century.

Over the years, large areas of marshland have been drained and are now under cultivation. Today some broads, such as Ranworth Broad in the Bure Valley and Surlingham Broad in the Yare Valley, cover less than half the area they covered in the 1840s. Holiday-makers can be seen everywhere in the summer now, but this was not the case one hundred and fifty years ago. In those days nobody knew the marshes and waterways better than the people who lived there; the men who sailed the keels and wherries, or other freight-carrying craft, the marshmen, the reed cutters and eel catchers, to mention but a few, knew the best places to conceal contraband in this remote and sometimes bleak landscape.

Many marshland smugglers preferred to hide their goods in the natural cover of the reed beds or among the alders and willows, where there was less risk of discovery than in buildings. Although mills, barns and houses were used to hide contraband, they could often be seen for miles and were much more accessible than many of the hiding places where natural cover was used. It was not surprising, with smuggling vessels landing cargoes almost every night, and some-

The Norfolk Broads
The broads and rivers were extensively used by smugglers

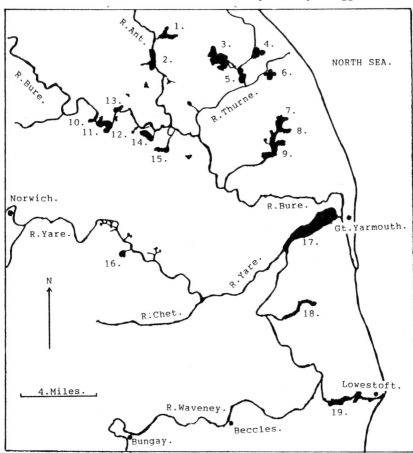

Main Broads

1. Sutton Broad	8. Rollesby Broad	15. South Walsham Broad
2. Barton Broad	9. Filby Broad	16. Rockland Broad
3. Hickling Broad	10. Wroxham Broad	17. Breydon Water
4. Horsey Mere	11. Hoveton Great Broad	18. Fritton Decoy
5. Heigham Sound	12. Salhouse Bridge	19. Oulton Broad
6. Martham Broad	13. Hoveton Little Broad	
7. Ormesby Bridge	14. Ranworth Broad	

Horsey Mere and its reed-beds.
Smugglers often hid their vessels and contraband among the reeds
before transporting them inland.

times in the daytime, that large quantities of contraband were being carried inland and many temporary hiding places had to be found to conceal it. Early seizures of contraband in the Broads area were reported in 1736 on Horsey Mere and in 1749 at Ranworth Broad.

The first of these seizures took place in January 1736. Captain Stewart, a dragoon officer, was a dinner guest at Sustead Hall, when two of his men arrived and informed him that they had seized 19 cwt. of tea on Horsey Mere and had taken it to Yarmouth Custom House, where they had been given a receipt for it. The tea had been landed from a Dutch dogger, a two-masted bluff-bowed fishing boat, on the beach near Horsey and taken to the Mere. It was the biggest seizure of tea made on that part of the Norfolk coast for some time.

In 1749, Robert Hagon kept the Woods End, a public house on the south bank of the River Yare at Bramerton, four and a half miles south-east of Norwich. Smugglers regularly made use of the Yare to transport their goods and were regular visitors to this pub. In spite of the penalties for harbouring smugglers, Hagon allowed them to stay on his premises. In December that year, five smugglers, three of them outlawed, were at the Woods End. Information of their whereabouts was passed to a customs officer at Beccles and, accompanied by a party of dragoons, he made his way to Bramerton, early one morning.

At 2 a.m. they raided the Woods End and arrested the smugglers and Robert Hagon. The outlawed smugglers were James Carbold alias 'Jiffling Jack', Charles Gowen alias the 'Papist of Beccles' and John Doe formerly of Norwich. The other two were Richard Parsons and John Balderoy, labourers from Lindsey and Barking Tye in Suffolk, who were later charged with assembling with others at Ranworth Broad the previous August and having in their possession foreign tea and brandy. Hagon was committed to Norwich Castle but was eventually released. However he was arrested again the following March for the same offence.

Woods End Tavern, Bramerton.
The inn of this name which stood here in the eighteenth century, was surrounded by customs officers and soldiers in 1749. The innkeeper and five smugglers were arrested.

Several other seizures were later reported in the press. They included one made at Horning, a village lying between the navigable rivers Bure and Ant, which was surrounded by marshland and fen. Two riding officers arrived in the village in August 1768 and searched the barn belonging to the public house near the ferry. They discovered two carts loaded with 80 half-ankers of brandy and geneva and 4 bags of tea, which they seized and transported to the Custom House at Great Yarmouth.

Three years later a seizure was made at Martham, a village on rising ground above the marshes, about nine and a half miles north-west of Yarmouth. Three customs officers, assisted by three dragoons, searched a barn and discovered 76 casks of brandy and geneva, containing 323 gallons, which they promptly seized.

Some excise officers from Yarmouth seized 149 half-ankers of geneva, 8 bags containing 216 lbs. of tea and a bag of rhubarb on the marshes between Horsey and Martham in June 1777. In those days the variety of rhubarb grown in China and imported via Turkey, was consumed in this country for medicinal purposes and was subject to duties.

Just north of the parish of Horstead is Mayton Bridge, which was built over the River Bure in the fifteenth century. It is a twin-arched brick-built structure with a strong central support. In 1779 navigation up the Bure to Aylsham was improved, and to assist the passage of large vessels, the river was diverted and another bridge built a short distance away. Today water passes under only one of the arches. However the western parapet of this bridge is very interesting, as it terminates at both ends with alcoves, supporting tiled roofs, similar to sentry boxes. They are thought to have been tollbooths as they over-look the road on the north and south approaches to the bridge. It is believed that these alcoves not only gave shelter to watchmen, but were later used by excise men watching the river for smugglers.

The many windmills throughout the Broads area were very useful when it came to storing contraband. A mill near Stalham Dyke was known to be a temporary hiding place for smuggled goods run between Horsey and Happisburgh, and the mill previously on the site of Horsey Mill was also used as a store house by smugglers. Grapes Mill near Potter Heigham was regularly stacked full of tobacco and this must have been the case with most of the marshland mills at some time or other.

The mills were also used to signal information to the smugglers. The millers would set the sails of their mills at certain angles over fifty square miles of flat marshes, to warn those involved with smuggling that a cargo had been run, or that revenue officers, or coastguards were patrolling the area. If the officers left Yarmouth to search a mill at Horsey, the smugglers would have been warned long before they

**Mayton Bridge, Horstead, on the old course of the Bure.
It was said locally that excisemen once made use of the strange
alcoves on the western parapet to watch the river.**

arrived. The millers set their mill sails upright in the form of a cross and one would signal to another across the miles of marshland; the warning would take as little as fifteen minutes to reach Horsey.

It is hardly surprising that the Broads were used by smugglers to sink crops of tubs just as they did in the sea; probably the tubs were easier to sink in fresh water than in salt water. Two such seizures by Brighton Silvers, the Yarmouth tide surveyor, at South Walsham Broad and in Runham parish, have already been mentioned. The tubs had to be sunk deep enough so that they could not be seen from the surface. It is known that tubs were sunk in Sutton Broad and it is thought that many of them were never recovered by the smugglers.

A large proportion of the contraband which passed through Broadland was bound for Norwich. It was common for smugglers to run their goods on the beach at Horsey under the cover of darkness, and carry them the short distance to the Mere, where they were loaded into wherries and other waiting craft. The vessels would then sail to Wroxham by the rivers Thurne and Bure, where they were unloaded into wagons and transported to Norwich. A report in the *Norwich Mercury* stated that on July 16th 1816, John Callow, the riding officer stationed at Winterton, had seized 77 casks of spirits concealed in a marshboat on the River Thurne.

Many wherrymen were involved in smuggling. After a run some smugglers in the Happisburgh neighbourhood would convey their goods to the little staithe at Stalham and load them aboard wherries bound for Norwich. Other wherry crews had every opportunity to obtain smuggled goods on their regular runs to Yarmouth, where ships' cargoes were transferred to them to be transported inland. It was easy for contraband to be slipped aboard the wherries unnoticed at such times. George Griffen of Ludham owned a wherry called *The Little Georgie*. He managed to smuggle goods successfully for some time before his vessel was seized and he was sent to prison.

In the mid-nineteenth century old Tom Rudd was a marshman and gamekeeper who lived on the banks of Hickling Broad. Many years earlier, his father had been a smuggler and when Tom was a boy he had gone on smuggling trips with him, sometimes with lace wound round his body under his clothes. They often sailed in a lugger, and after several successful trips, from which quite a lot of money was made, his father decided to give up the trade. However, he thought he would make one more voyage, which turned out to be disastrous. While they were at sea a fierce gale blew their vessel up the Thames and customs officers boarded her. The officers discovered contraband on board and they were all sent to gaol.

Much of the contraband run on the Suffolk coast was destined for Norwich. A considerable seizure of liquors was reported in Kessingland, by customs officers in March 1774. In this same area during the nineteenth century a gap in the cliffs between Pakefield and Kessingland called Crazy Mary's Hole was regularly used by smugglers when carrying contraband inland. There were one or two farmhouses not far from the gap, where the smugglers used to congregate and horses were kept in readiness to take cartloads of tubs down to the River Waveney, where wherries were waiting to take them by this river to the River Yare and on to Norwich.

Villages close to these rivers were well supplied with goods by the smugglers and stories of their activities are still told in some places. Claxton is a village on the banks of the River Yare. A story is told there of how Dutch smugglers used to leave their boats on the river and carry their goods up the loke beside the Post Office. A thatched cottage in the village was thought to have been used by smugglers as a storehouse for their goods.

About three miles north of the Waveney lie North and South Lopham. It is likely that people living in that area were supplied with smuggled goods which had been brought up the river. The following information was taken from a warrant issued for the arrest of a Lopham man. It did not state which village he came from. On May 27th 1786, three excise officers, James Lea, supervisor, Henry Coates and Samuel Christmas were assaulted and obstructed in the course of their duty by Thomas Cock the younger, an alehouse-keeper at Lopham. The warrant was issued for Cock's arrest by Francis Buller, one of the Judges of the Court of the King's Bench. He was to be bound by £100 surety or two sureties of £50 each, to appear in court. He was eventually arrested in November and taken before John Fenn, a magistrate, who committed him to Norwich Castle when he refused to find the necessary sureties.

One region where surprisingly few smuggling incidents were reported in the eighteenth and nineteenth centuries, is Breckland. This area extends over south-west Norfolk and north-west Suffolk, covering an area of about four hundred square miles, two hundred and fifty-three of which are in Norfolk. In the eighteenth century it

The Peddars' Way, once regularly used by smugglers when carrying goods from the Norfolk coast.

was virtually a treeless waste, mile after mile of sandy heathland. Although the area includes the towns of Thetford and Swaffham, it was thinly populated. Good roads across these dry, arid lands were few and, being hedgeless, were often blocked by drifting snow in the winter, and wind-blown sand at other times. Two of the oldest roads running through Breckland are the Icknield Way and Peddar's Way. The former consists of a series of trackways running along the chalk ridge which begins at the Wash in north-west Norfolk, and terminates in Wessex on the south coast. East of this is Peddar's Way, which was on a road built by the Romans from the Colchester area to the north Norfolk coast near Hunstanton.

It is thought that smugglers made regular use of these old routes and a long stretch of the Icknield Way, passing through Bodney Warren into what is now the Stanford Battle Area, is in fact named 'Smugglers' Road'. The village of Stanford is on this ancient route, which also passes through the town of Thetford. Contraband was seized at both these places according to eighteenth century newspaper reports.

Mansell and Webb, two Thetford excise officers, were reported in the *Norwich Mercury,* April 1781, to have seized a hundredweight of

Smuggling Routes through Breckland

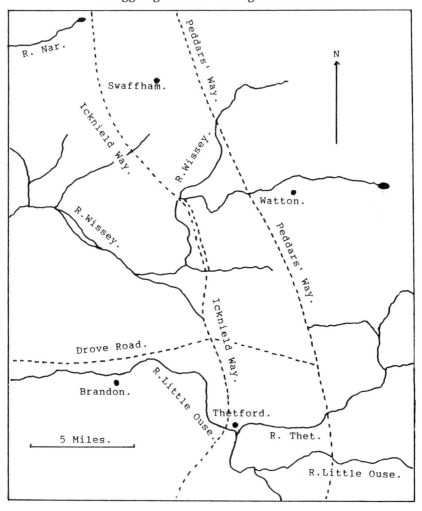

**The Smugglers' Road across Bodney Warren,
part of the Icknield Way.**
From *In Breckland Wilds by* Rainbird Clarke

Congoe tea at Stanford Cock, a public house in the village on the south side of the River Wissey, about six miles south-west of Watton. The officers conveyed the tea to the Excise Office at Thetford.

The following month a man and woman found in a brick kiln near Thetford 11 half-ankers of gin, which were thought to have been hidden there by a man whose cart had broken down the night before. The couple who found the gin took it to their house in Thetford, but Mr Mansell of the Excise Office had been informed. He went to the house and seized the gin. As the gin was being taken to the Excise Office, a man, described as an idle spectator, cut the cord securing two tubs to the shoulders of the carrier and staved one in the street.

Not all smugglers restricted themselves to a particular region and some travelled many miles about the country and were well known in several counties. One night in September 1785, two noted smugglers and horse thieves named Joseph Moore, alias Gosden, and Robert Sutton, alias Platford, stole a black gelding and a black mare from Hanworth Common in Middlesex. Moore was well known in Norfolk, Suffolk and Essex and it was therefore no surprise when the gelding was later recovered from a person living near Norwich who had purchased it. Five other horses taken from the Common on the same night were also recovered at various places in Norfolk. One was found in King Street in Norwich and the others were found at Cringleford, Bixley, Yarmouth and Great Snoring. It would appear that Moore and Sutton spent some of their time in or near Norwich, and they were eventually recognised in that area in May 1786. They were chased as far as Trowse where, with the assistance of some constables, they were arrested. A Yarmouth man named Waller, one of Moore's relations, was detained in Odiham gaol in Hampshire where he gave evidence against him. Moore and Sutton were eventually sent to Newgate to await trial.

Some smugglers were so well organised that they were able to carry on their business in places many miles apart. In 1832 the Phillips brothers of Ipswich owned the *Mary*, a twenty-eight ton cutter. One of the brothers also owned three houses, one at Bramford in Suffolk, one in London, which he used as his headquarters for smuggling, and the other at Blakeney in Norfolk, where he was known as Barry. It would appear that the brothers sold the bulk of their contraband in London.

There is little doubt that smuggling took place in every part of Norfolk, as was probably the case in the country as a whole. Wherever there were customers, there were smugglers plying their trade. The landscape of the regions in the county varied considerably, and provided many hiding places for contraband. Norfolk people from all levels of society enjoyed their tipple, smoke or some of the other commodities that came ashore on the Norfolk coast and were carried along the ancient trails or waterways into the heart of the county.

A selection of seizures reported in Norfolk 1736-1824

Date	Contraband	Where taken
1736	Brandy, 14 gals. Tea, 690 lbs.	North Walsham
1748	Tea, 1 ton	Eccles, Portland's Gap
1774	Geneva, 26 half-ankers Brandy, 1 half-anker	Hickling
1774	Liquor, 46 tubs	Woodbastwick
1774	Gin, 130 half-ankers	Great Yarmouth
1775	Geneva, 60 half-ankers	Morston, barn

1775	Geneva, rum, tea, silks, firearms, gunlocks, nankeens, cards, china etc.	Weybourne
1776	Geneva, 144 half-ankers	Acle
1776	Geneva, 10 half-ankers	Hempstead
1777	Geneva, 21 casks	Kelling
1778	Tea & Geneva, several cartloads	Harleston
1779	Geneva, 84 half-ankers	Stalham, vault
1779	Geneva, 141 half-ankers	Pulham St Mary, cottage
1782	Brandy, 43 half-ankers Geneva, 44 half-ankers	Ringstead
1783	Geneva, 10 casks	Southrepps, on road
1783	Geneva, 23 casks	Trunch, barn
1783	Tea 450 lbs. Rum, brandy, Geneva, 39 half-ankers	West Rudham Church tower
1784	Liquor, 8 tubs. Tea, 2 bags	Setch
1787	Foreign spirits, 150 casks	Trimingham
1797	Spirits, 92 casks	Thorpe Market
1805	Geneva, 80 gals. Brandy, 4 gals.	Melton
1819	Cart loaded with spirits	Kenninghall
1824	Geneva, 32 half-ankers Tobacco, 16 casks. Tea, 6 casks	Gunton, vault in plantation
1826	Cart loaded with 21 casks of spirits and tobacco	Briston

St Peter's Church, West Rudham.
There was a notable seizure here in January 1783

10. Smuggling Tales

Information can be found in official records about smuggling that took place several centuries ago. However, information passed down verbally and eventually written down can also be important. This information mainly takes the form of smuggling stories, which can be put into three categories: ghost stories, travelling stories and true stories that originated locally.

In the eighteenth and nineteenth centuries, people were much more superstitious than they are today and smugglers either made up ghost stories, or made use of existing ones to keep people indoors at night and so reduce the risk of them being seen as they went about their business. This may account for the many areas round the Norfolk coast where Black Shuck, the large ghostly dog, is said to have been seen. The Norfolk Shuck (the other East Anglian counties have their own Black Shucks) was said to be as black as ebony and his fiendish howls could be heard above the wildest gales. It was a popular belief in Norfolk that nobody could set eyes on Black Shuck and live. Smugglers are said to have put lanterns on large dogs and let them run through the darkness, so that people who saw them thought they had seen Black Shuck.

A smuggling gang that regularly ran their cargoes on the coast north of Happisburgh also realised the value of a little ghostly acting to keep prying eyes away from their operations. This gang chose an old manor house, supposedly haunted, as a hiding place for their smuggled goods. One of the gang dressed up in ghostly garb and was said to 'perform mysterious antics', in order to frighten away the villagers and other people who might show an interest in the house.

A ghost story was told in this area that was said to date from the early nineteenth century. Apparently the people of Happisburgh were very concerned by the frequent appearance in the main street of the village of a ghostly apparition which usually came from the direction of Cart Gap in the cliffs. It was legless and its head hung down its back, attached only to its neck by a strip of skin. It was dressed in seaman's clothes and carried a strange bundle in its arms. One night two farmers encountered this ghost and followed it until it came to a well. They saw it throw the bundle it was carrying into the well and then it vanished. Later when the men told their story, it was decided to search the well. When it was searched a pair of human legs were found in a sack, tied up at the mouth, and the legless body of a seaman, dressed exactly like the ghost, was also discovered. A pistol thought to have belonged to the deceased was also brought up.

Some days later a large amount of blood was found near Cart Gap, and it was thought that the man in the well had been murdered there. A pistol was found in a nearby shed, just like the one discovered in the well. Some gold coins were picked up and the remains of some empty Schiedam bottles were found nearby. It was thought that a number of Dutch smugglers had landed on the coast, quarrelled, fought among themselves and one of them was killed. The victim's legs were cut off and thrown down the well with his body.

Whether there was ever a body in a well or whether this tale was put about by smugglers is not known, but there seems to be no factual evidence to support it.

The travelling stories are likely to have been true, but were so popular that they have been attributed to various parts of the country and their place of origin lost. One such story was recorded in connection with the Overstrand area of the north Norfolk coast. A revenue officer called at a cottage where he suspected contraband had been hidden. An old lady sat knitting by the fire, while he searched the cottage. She remained seated throughout the officer's fruitless search and only after he had gone did she venture to stand up and reveal that her seat had actually been a keg of smuggled spirits, which she had managed to conceal under the folds of her dress. Versions of this story have been attributed to Suffolk and Kent and it seems that this tale has travelled and its place of origin is now obscure.

The third group of stories are true and originated locally. They often give the names of people and places that can be traced today. These stories survive because they contain an element of humour, which has led to them being repeated and eventually written down. They are the most important of the three types of stories, because they show people's attitudes to smuggling and smugglers.

In his book, *Old Norfolk Inns,* published in 1888, E. A. Culley recorded a smuggling story involving the landlord of the Feathers Inn, Holt, and a doctor living in the town some sixty years earlier. Culley took care to leave out their names, but there is little doubt that this was a family story passed on to him, because research has shown that

The Feathers, Holt, where Martha, the cook, hid contraband in her oven.

the landlord of the Feathers in 1828 was William Culley.

The story began when the doctor arrived home one evening, tired and hungry after spending most of the day travelling about the countryside, visiting his patients. After he had finished his meal, he noticed a hamper standing in the corner of the room. He asked his housekeeper where it had come from. She said that two men dressed like fishermen had left it earlier in the day, implying that it contained lobsters and that the doctor knew all about it. The doctor was surprised and said that he knew nothing about it, but as he frequently received presents from his patients, he thought that it might be one. However, when he opened the hamper he found that it contained spirits, cigars and tobacco. There was no doubt that they were all contraband, and the doctor was well aware what the consequences would be if smuggled goods were found on his premises.

The doctor thought he knew who had sent him the hamper, because among his poorer patients was a family in which the father and sons were fishermen and he was often called upon to treat them for injuries, which, in his opinion, were more likely to have been caused by smuggling than fishing. This family had not paid the doctor's last bill, and the wife had said they could not pay it all at once, but they would make it up to him. As he inspected the hamper, he felt sure this was the smuggler's mode of paying their bill. His first impulse was to send the hamper back, but he knew that the family would deny all knowledge of smuggling transactions, so he decided to destroy the hamper and its contents, telling his housekeeper that it contained, not lobster, but specimens he required.

However, before he could destroy it, he received a badly written note warning him that somebody had informed the authorities that contraband goods had been taken to his house, and it was likely that his premises would be searched. He sent for his gardener and gave him some important instructions before leaving for the Feathers Inn, where he and the landlord, William Culley, a lifelong friend, went into a private room. The doctor told him the story of the hamper and asked him if he would hide it at the Feathers. The landlord refused to do this, pointing out that although it would be serious if contraband was found on the doctor's premises, it would be doubly so if it was found on the premises of a licensed victualler. They discussed dumping the hamper in the sea, but dared not in case the doctor was being watched. Telling the excisemen the truth about how he came by the hamper and who he thought it came from would also be too risky, as the doctor thought he might be murdered by smugglers on one of his lonely rides to see his patients. Still undecided the doctor went to see Old Martha, the cook at the Feathers, who had once been in the service of his father and later himself. In spite of her age she was a dapper little woman in her neat print dress and high mob cap. She warmly welcomed the doctor who prescribed for the aches and pains she complained of, and after some discussion he went home.

The following morning while he was having breakfast, the doctor's housekeeper informed him that two excise officers wished to see him. When they entered the room, the older officer, whom the doctor knew and liked, told him that his younger colleague had received private information that contraband goods had been brought to the doctor's house and he was sorry, but it was his duty to search for them. The officers were shown round by the housekeeper and they carried out a thorough search before leaving empty-handed.

Shortly after, the younger excise officer, who had been sent specially to the district to watch for smuggling, received secret information concerning the Feathers Inn. He informed his colleague and they went to the inn. The landlord was very surprised when the officers told him why they had come and pointed out that they had examined his stock the previous week and that he had added nothing since then. However the officers told him that they were obliged to search the inn. As the landlord accompanied the officers in their search, he suddenly remembered the doctor's hamper, and began to feel uneasy, half expecting the doctor's contraband to turn up in some nook or cranny; but to his great relief nothing was found and only the kitchen remained to be searched. As they entered the kitchen the landlord, knowing that it did not take much to upset Martha, quietly told her that some foolish person had told the officers that there may be smuggled goods on the premises and she must let them look round.

Martha did not answer; her attention was directed to the young officer who was turning over her stores in a manner that roused her temper. She asked him in a loud voice if he thought she was a pirate and called him a 'Jack-a-dandy fellow'. She had been making pastry and half a dozen pies stood ready to go in the oven. She put one in the oven and closed the door with a loud bang that made the exciseman, who had his back to her, jump. In went another and another pie until they were all in the oven, and Martha's anger had risen to fever pitch. She stood by the side of the great old-fashioned stove before the fire in which savoury joints were roasting, and her home-made bread, carefully covered with a cloth, was in the reflector to rise. The exciseman, who had succeeded in reducing Martha's kitchen into a state of confusion, now approached the oven to examine it. This was too much for Martha's patience; she took the red-hot poker out of the fire and flourished it close to the astonished officer, who quickly stepped backwards. She ordered him out of the kitchen and called him a 'born idiot'. As she advanced, the officer was forced to retreat to the door and the landlord and the other officer, although almost convulsed with laughter, managed to persuade her not to follow him out of the kitchen. Martha's enemy was very angry, but the landlord apologised for his cook's behaviour, and invited the two officers to luncheon in the bar; the matter therefore ended happily as far as they were concerned.

The landlord left the officers at their lunch and went to see Martha. He expected to find her still angry, but no, she was chuckling to herself with great satisfaction when she informed him that the doctor's contraband was in the oven. She had told the doctor that she would take care of it for him and she had known that the officers were looking for it. Soon the officers left the inn, little suspecting that Martha had tricked them. She had been baking with a cold oven; the contraband was at the back of it and the pies were at the front. The doctor had entrusted the contraband to his gardener to take into Martha's charge, before his conversation with the landlord, probably anticipating what his decision would be, and he wished to put him on his guard in case the excise officers should visit the inn - as they did.

The landlord did not inquire who removed the contraband from the inn, nor did he wish to know, so long as it was off his premises. Some time later, having business with the doctor, he called upon him one evening, and before leaving had some Hollands and cigars. Having sampled them he asked if they were part of the contents of the hamper. The doctor replied that they had fairly earned them, as they had been given a precious fright. However, he wondered where the hamper had come from, because the people he suspected had sent it had paid their bill and never mentioned it.

Inns were generally treated with suspicion by excise officers, and rightly so, as inns selling spirits on which duty had been paid found it difficult to compete with inns selling smuggled spirits. Information from informers, many with the hope of obtaining a reward if it led to a conviction, was quickly acted upon.

In the early years of the nineteenth century, the excisemen suspected that smuggled spirits were hidden at the lonely Cherry Tree Inn at Plumstead, just over five miles from the north Norfolk coast. The inn stood back from the road about a quarter of a mile from the village, an ideal place to conceal smuggled spirits. When the excise officers arrived, the innkeeper was taken completely by surprise and had no chance to remove the spirits from his premises. However Nannie Brett, who had been cooking a meal, met them at the door and the odour of roast ducks did not escape their attention. Encouraged by Nannie, they decided to have a meal before they searched the inn and were shown into the front room where they dined on roast ducks and consumed a quantity of ale. They were delighted when Nannie brought them a bottle of wine, which of course prolonged their meal. Meanwhile, several strong men slipped quietly into the Cherry Tree and removed barrel after barrel and hid them from prying eyes. When the officers finally finished their meal, they searched the inn, found nothing and rode away with nothing but praise for their hostess.

Major Charles Loftus of Stiffkey, in *My Life 1815-1849,* described how he witnessed contraband being run at Wells about 1818. He observed a cutter standing off the shore for a time and then a sudden rush for the water's edge by a crowd of people. Several light carts were then driven furiously across the sand. A customs officer called upon him in the King's name to assist as a cargo of brandy and tobacco was being run, and the officer's party was outnumbered. Loftus and three friends were mounted and, forming a line, advanced to the scene where he saw men from his own village, including the baker who was struggling with one of the preventive men. The 'cavalry' then charged at full gallop into the mêlée and scattered the crowd in all directions. In passing, Loftus gave the smuggler baker a whack with his whip for old acquaintance sake, and so the officers were saved from a beating, but they only managed to seize 6 tubs, the smugglers getting away with the rest.

The *Norwich Mercury,* January 4th 1823, reported the following story under the title 'Ludicrous Seizure'.

'A short time since, an information was laid, that sixty casks of gin were buried in the park of a great Norfolk commoner, upon which hint two officers of Excise accompanied the two informers to the grave of the tubs, and speedily raised their spirits. Rather at a loss for a conveyance, they pressed into service the tumbrel of a neighbouring farmer, which they loaded with their liquid treasure, and mounting themselves, started in tip-top spirits for the adjacent receipt of Customs. - How frail are all the hopes of man? Exulting in possession, it never occurred to these worthies that linch pins are sometimes taken from the wheels, until convinced of the fact, by finding the cart, the tubs, the Excisemen, and informers, whelmed in one prodigious ruin. On re-collecting the stock, some tubs were found much injured by the fall, and the contents of several others had sunk in the barren sand. The remainder being secured the party resumed their journey, but on starting, Old Dobbin released, as if by magic, from the ties which bound him to the tumbrel, walked quietly forward, leaving his cargo of cares behind him, and the whole party of gin and gentlemen were again precipitated into the road. We have not learned what other impediments presented themselves to the broad arrows of these resurrection-men, but it seems quite certain, from the mishaps we have recorded that on the Eastern Coast of Norfolk, it is not always safe to meddle with those "who call spirits from the vasty deep"'.

A smuggling story which was told by a farmer's wife was published some years later in the *Norwich Mercury*, July 21st 1923. It concerned a smuggler named Drury Ford, who lived in the village of Edgefield south of Holt. He was a very mean character; he even made a hole in his frozen pond and concealed it with straw, so that it might catch boys who came to slide. One cold winter night when snow was falling, Drury and another man went to collect some smuggled spirits. As they returned home, they sampled the spirits, which resulted in Drury's companion falling out of the cart and Drury becoming thoroughly intoxicated. The horse, which was left to find its own way home, became thirsty and went to drink at the hole in his master's pond. While the horse was drinking, Drury fell into the pond and was drowned. The horse returned to his stable and, finding nobody to unharness it, neighed piteously. In the morning Drury's neighbours heard his horse neighing and, seeing it was still harnessed, followed the wheel tracks in the snow and learned the smuggler's fate.

The following tale appeared in a history of Overstrand and Sidestrand, (George Beckett, 1899). One night a boat was run silently on to the beach at Overstrand and a gang of smugglers began to unload its cargo quickly and quietly. Suddenly an alarm was raised and the men dispersed, each laden with a keg. One man hurried across the beach and scaled the precipitous cliff, arriving near the top breathless. Suddenly a voice called him from the cliff top and offered to help him with his load. He accepted the offer and passed the keg up; soon the keg was safe on the top of the cliff. Having gained his breath the perspiring man scrambled to the top and looked around for his helper, but the man with the friendly voice had disappeared and, anxious to relieve the unfortunate smuggler of his burden, had taken the keg with him.

In an article entitled 'Smuggling in Norfolk', published in the *Eastern Daily Press*, December 29th 1926, a story once told by an old fisherman was related. He had said that a 'hoveller', an unlicensed pilot or boatman, was used to running his cargoes at Happisburgh, Sea Palling, or the south end of Corton Cliff, and on one occasion a preventive man concealed himself and watched the proceedings.

However he was discovered by the smugglers and seized. They pushed his head into a rabbit's burrow and drove a stake between his legs so that he was helpless and unable to give any alarm. The old fisherman, who was there, went on to say that when the boat came in, the sea was so rough that it broke up, but its cargo was carried safely away.

Wherries in Yarmouth Harbour.
These vessels were used to smuggle large quantities of contraband along the inland waterways to Norwich and other places.

The Norfolk Broads was the setting for another smuggling story which was told by Roy Clark in his book, *Black Sailed Traders,* in 1961. The story began one dark night when two wagon loads of contraband were put on to a wherry near Yarmouth to be transported to Norwich. The hatches were put on and she slid quietly downstream to Breydon Water. The wherry was crewed by three brothers named Royall. When they were nearing the mouth of the River Yare, they noticed a sail astern, and soon realised that they were being followed by a Custom House cutter. The officers had probably received information concerning the run and were on the lookout for vessels carrying contraband.

The wherry sailed up the River Yare with the cutter following, the officers knowing that she could not give them the slip as a vessel could at sea. Sooner or later she would have to stop and the officers would be able to board her. When the brothers reached Thorpe, they took the wherry's sail down and moored her near the church. The customs officers were so close behind that the Royalls had no chance to escape and were arrested. As soon as the brothers had been taken away, the customs officers began to unload the wherry, which took some time. When they had finished, they went to refresh themselves at a nearby public house.

While they were there, some of the Royalls' friends slipped aboard the wherry, raised her sail and set off up the river. When the officers returned to where the wherry had been moored they were surprised to find that she was no longer there. Then they noticed the top of her sail disappearing into the distance. They ran to their cutter to give chase, but found that she had been tampered with and they were unable to raise her sail. The wherry was taken to some lonely part of the broads and sunk. Her location was never discovered by the customs officers and she was therefore saved from being sold or burnt, the usual fate of captured smuggling vessels. The Royall brothers spent a year in prison and when they were released raised their wherry and were eventually seen trading again between Norwich and Yarmouth.

Any tale which embarrassed the customs or excise officers would be remembered for many years by local people and passed on from one generation to another. One such tale, written down in the later years of the nineteenth century, related to the north Norfolk coast. It concerned a field in Sidestrand, known locally as Hickman's Folly. This field ran from the brow of Hungry Hill to the mill. Many years earlier Hickman, as an officer in the Coastguard, had attempted to seize a load of contraband being conveyed along the narrow lane beside the mill by a gang of smugglers. However, he and his men were overpowered in the struggle and to prevent them from summoning assistance they were firmly tied to the trees growing beside the lane. Hickman and his men were eventually discovered and released and the adjoining field has been known as Hickman's Folly ever since.

A story was once related by John Buck, an East Tuddenham man who died in December 1928 aged 80, about his grandfather who at one time had in his possession a tub of smuggled gin. Someone informed the preventive officers about it, and when he heard this he quickly took it to Fran's Green, where Billy Atterton lived. Billy and his wife were in bed suffering from smallpox and they allowed Buck to hide the tub under their bed. Soon after this, the preventive officers arrived and dug up Buck's garden; they also dragged the nearby ponds but could find nothing and eventually left empty-handed. When Buck felt it was safe to retrieve his gin he went to Billy Atterton's house only to find that Billy and his wife had drunk the lot. Billy's house was known locally as the Spy Glass, because all the roads to Norwich could be seen through a peephole in the roof.

The final tale concerns smuggling in the Gorleston area in the eighteenth century. Writing under the pseudonym Athol Forbes in 1909, the Reverend Forbes Phillips, the Vicar of Gorleston, related the following story about one of his predecessors. The vicarage had originally been constructed with large cellars where smuggled goods were often stored. It was said that an underground passage once connected these cellars to a landing stage. The plan for the vicarage to be built in this way was hatched by the vicar in the late eighteenth century.

One night in the autumn of 1789, a cargo of contraband was being run. The local revenue officers had been supplied with false information and were following it up some distance away, leaving the coast clear for the smugglers. Scouts were posted along the cliff top by the smugglers to warn them of the approach of the revenue officers while they were running their cargo. Men were busy loading pack horses on the beach and one tub had been staved to allow those working to have a quick drink. A tall man with a lantern was quietly giving instructions to the men who were helping to check and carry away the contraband.

Suddenly a stranger appeared on the beach and demanded to know what was going on. When he realised he was witnessing goods being run by a large number of smugglers, he began to shout loudly for a magistrate, and he then demanded to know where he could find a clergyman. A man passed him carrying a cask and took pains to point out the vicar, standing a short distance away - holding the lantern.

11. The Decline of Smuggling

By the 1830s, the Coastguard had become a highly efficient service and the beaches were watched so closely that it was almost impossible for smugglers to run a cargo without being detected. Smuggling declined dramatically and there were only occasional reports of seizures of contraband on the Norfolk coast at this time. One incident was reported in November 1832, when the officers of the Preventive Service stationed at Brancaster seized a large tub-boat, containing 5,565 lbs of tobacco and about 650 gallons of brandy and geneva, all of which was taken to the Custom House at Wells-next-the-Sea.

One of the last big runs reported on the Norfolk coast was that which took place at Kelling in February 1833; this run was foiled by Lieutenant Howes and his men. (See page 103)

In 1834, the collector at the port of King's Lynn reported that to his knowledge there had been no increase in smuggling in his district, and no contraband goods had been run for some time. However an anonymous letter signed 'Fair Play' was sent to the Board of Commissioners from King's Lynn in 1839. The letter stated that large quantities of spirits were being smuggled into the port in ships laden with timber from the Baltic. The letter cited a particular ship named the *Fate,* stating that her master had been selling liquor, tobacco and cigars for a number of years. It also claimed that the officers in the Customs at the port were closely related to the crews who smuggled these goods and were often bribed with liquor and tobacco.

The Collector was ordered to act on the information supplied in the letter and a watch was kept on the *Fate*. She was eventually searched and illegal spirits and tobacco were found on board. Her master was later fined £100 for smuggling, although he claimed that he was innocent and that the goods found on board his vessel had been put there by the crew.

Some of the smuggled goods coming through the port of King's Lynn at this time were conveyed inland by various means. In July 1836 Mr J. Gotobed, one of the proprietors of the Lynn Coach, was fined £50 'for having driven away the coach after it had been seized by His Majesty's Officers of Excise for conveying contraband spirits'.

In the 1840s Britain embarked on an era of free trade; tariffs were greatly reduced or abolished altogether on a large number of commodities. It was no longer worth the risks involved in running cargoes on the beaches and the public no longer looked sympathetically upon the smuggler. He was now seen as a criminal who robbed the community.

Although the Revenue Services had become more successful against the smugglers, it was free trade that really put a stop to smuggling in tea, wines and silks. The only goods which remained worth smuggling were spirits and tobacco. A report concerning the tobacco trade, issued in 1884, showed that tobacco could be purchased anywhere in the United Kingdom for 2s. 6d. per pound, while the duty alone was 3s. 2d. Two foreign ports from which tobacco was smuggled into Britain were Flushing and Nieuwpoort, and there was evidence that establishments had been set up in those ports for packaging tobacco for the smuggling trade. Large quantities of smuggled goods were brought ashore by ships' crews. Whole crews on some ships smuggled tobacco and were deliberately paid low wages because they had the opportunity to make money by smuggling.

The Commander-General of the Coastguard, Captain Hornsby, said that if tobacco smuggling was to cease the duty would have to be taken off altogether. He went on to say that the fishermen on the Kent and Sussex coasts would carry on smuggling, however small the duty, because they had better facilities than the fair trader. Their living was made by working in boats; they had no port dues or lights to pay and did not incur any of the expenses of waiting upon merchant ships. Therefore, even if the duty on tobacco was very low, they could still undersell the fair trader.

This of course was also true of fishermen on other coasts, including Norfolk. In 1850 a wherry was searched at Yarmouth and nearly 650 lbs. of a superior leaf tobacco were discovered on board. It had just been transferred from a small Cromer fishing boat.

In May that year, the revenue cutter *Prince of Wales,* under the command of Lieutenant John Allen, stopped and boarded a vessel named the *Sea Flower* of Hull, off Happisburgh. She was found to be carrying 122 bales of tobacco, containing 50 lbs. each, the duty upon which amounted to £900. The vessel and her cargo were confiscated.

Although the smuggling of spirits and tobacco had been radically reduced, these commodities were still to be smuggled into the country for many years. The following extract is from a 'Statement concerning smuggling' in the Customs' Report for the year ending March 31st 1891.

Quantities Seized

Year	Tobacco	Spirits	No. of Convictions	Penalties recovered
1882	25,653 pounds	432 gallons	1,516	£3,529
1891	16,753 pounds	239 gallons	4,704	£8,126

It was noted that the larger seizures occurred for the most part on the shores of the Humber.

Tobacco smuggling continued well into the 20th century. A well-organised gang of smugglers was broken up when a large seizure of tobacco was made at King's Lynn in 1935. A chartered vessel, the *Hawarden Castle,* was searched at the port and over 1,000 lbs. of tobacco was discovered under her cargo. When the captain's cabin was searched, documents were found which were written in a complicated code. These gave information about the tobacco and the names of the customers. The smugglers had been in the habit of loading their goods into a rowing boat at night and taking them to a storehouse up river. From here they were transported to their customers in Manchester and Leeds. The gang had successfully used this system for more than three years. It was stated in the press that this was a highly-organised, lucrative business and that if it was to be suppressed, smugglers should be sent to gaol for a long stretch, rather than the maximum sentence of six months allowed by the law.

Smuggling is not, of course, an occupation of the past but still continues today. Whenever people think that a commodity is profitable enough to smuggle, they are prepared to take the risks involved. Modern smugglers deal in a variety of things from wrist-watches to people, but one of the most profitable commodities to smuggle is drugs. Just how many commodities are smuggled into Norfolk is not known. As with the cargo-runners of the past, little is known about goods successfully run. One thing is certain though - there are no longer pitched battles between revenue officers, soldiers and smugglers on the Norfolk coast, or in other parts of the county.

Bibliography

Reference has been made throughout this book to weekly editions of the contemporary local newspapers, the *Norwich Mercury* 1725-1840 and the *Norfolk Chronicle* 1769-1840. Other sources are listed here chapter by chapter.

Chapter 1
Acts of the Privy Council of England, New Series Vols. I – XI, 1542-1580.
Calendar of Close Rolls, 1272-1446.
Calendar of Fine Rolls, 1369-1730.
Calendar of Inquisitions Miscellaneous, Vol. IV, 1377 – 1388.
Calendar of Patent Rolls, 1324 – 1422.
Royal Letters, Henry IV, Vol. II, 1405-1413
Calendar of State Papers Domestic, Vol. VII, 1601-1603 with addenda 1547-1565.
Calendar of Treasury Books, Vols. I to XXXII, 1660 –1718
Calendar of Treasury Books and Papers, 1714 – 1745.
Hillen, Henry James, *The History of King's Lynn* (1978).
Williams, Neville, *Contraband Cargoes* (1959).

Chapter 2
Calendar of Treasury Books, Vols. I to XXXII, 1660 – 1718.
Calendar of Treasury Books and Papers, 1714 – 1745.
Gentleman's Magazine, Vol. 4 1734, and Vol. 8 1738.
Benham, Harvey, *The Smugglers' Century*.
Plumb, J.H., *Men and Places* (1963).
Smith, Graham, *Something to Declare* (1980).
Williams, Neville, *Contraband Cargoes* (1959).
Young, Rachel, article in *Bygones 5* (1980).

Chapter 3
Harper, Charles G. *The Smugglers* (1909).
Smith, Graham, *Something to Declare* (1980).
Williams, Neville, *Contraband Cargoes* (1959)

Chapter 4
Mackie, Charles, *Norfolk Annals*, Vol. 1 1801-1851.
Woodforde, Revd James, *The Diary of a Country Parson*, Vol. 1, edited by James Beresford. (1935)

Chapter 5
Benham, Harvey, *Once upon a Tide* (1971).
Gentleman's Magazine, Vol. 19, 1749.
Ketton-Cremer, R.W. *Felbrigg: the story of a house* (1962).
Phillipson, David, *Smuggling, A History 1700-1900* (1973).
White, William, *Norfolk Directory 1845.*
Williams, Neville *Contraband Cargoes* (1959).

Chapter 6

Mackie, Charles, *Norfolk Annals*, Vol. 1, 1801 – 1851.

Phillipson, David, *Smuggling, A History* 1700-1900 (1973).

Rose, June, *Elizabeth Fry, a Biography* (1980).

Shore, H.N. *Smuggling Days and Smuggling Ways* (1892).

Chapter 7

Acts of the Privy Council of England, Vol. 1 1542-1547.

Beckett, George, *The Vale of Health or Overstrand and Sidestrand Past and Present* (1899).

Dutt, W.A. *The Norfolk and Suffolk Coast* (1909).

Gentleman's Magazine, Vol. 4 1734.

Harper, Charles, *The Smugglers* (1909).

Marcon, W.H. *Reminiscences of a Norfolk Parson* (1927).

Young, Arthur, *A General View of Agriculture of the County of Norfolk* (1804).

Chapter 8

Mackie, Charles, *Norfolk Annals*, Vol. 1 1801 – 1851 (1901).

Ready, Oliver G. *Life and Sport on the Norfolk Broads* (1910).

Smith, Graham, *Something to Declare*(1980).

Woodforde, Revd James, *The Diary of a Country Parson*, 5 vols. 1758-1802, edited by James Beresford (1935).

Chapter 9

Anderson, Verily, *The Northrepps Grandchildren* (1979).

Defoe, Daniel, *Tour Through the Eastern Counties* (1949).

Ketton-Cremer, R.W. *Country Neighbourhood* (1951).

Stacy, John, (printer*) Norfolk Tour 1829*, Vol. 1 (1829).

Millican, Percy, *A History of Horstead and Stanninghall, Norfolk* (1937).

Ready, Oliver G. *Life and Sport on the Norfolk Broads* (1910).

Chapter 10

Beckett, George, *The Vale of Health or Overstrand and Sidestrand Past and Present* (1899).

Clark, Roy, *Black Sailed Traders* (1972).

Culley, E.A. *Old Norfolk Inns* (1888).

Dutt, W.A. *The Norfolk and Suffolk Coast* (1909).

Loftus, Charles, *My Life from 1815-1849* (1877).

Thompson, Leonard P. *Smugglers of the Suffolk Coast* (1975).

Woodforde, Revd James, *The Diary of a Country Parson*. 5 vols. 1797-1802, edited by James Beresford (1935).

Chapter 11

Jarvis, Stan, *Smuggling in East Anglia 1700 – 1840* (1987).

Mackie, Charles, *Norfolk Annals* Vol. 1 1801-1851 (1901)

Smith, Graham, *Something to Declare* (1980).

Index of Names and Places

Entries in italics are the names of sailing vessels. Unless otherwise indicated the places listed are in Norfolk.

Abbot, Thomas, 55
Abinger, Lord, 131
Acle, 49, 152
Aldeburgh, Suff. 78, 93
Alderney, 77
Alderson, Steward, 70
Allen, Lieut. John, 165
Ames, Joseph, 46
Andrews, Mary, 41
Andrews, Richard, 70, 125
Ant, River, 143
Antingham, 121
Antwerp, Belgium, 14
Argus, 74, 75
Atterton, Billy, 163
Aylsham, 55, 144
Baconsthorpe, 104
Bacton, 9, 59, 77, 137
Badger, 108
Bailey, John, 25
Baker, 75
Balderoy, John, 38, 143
Ballard, Joseph, 100, 102
Barber, Thomas, 44
Barking Tye, Suff. 143
Barton, James 103
Bathurst, Richard, 24
Bawdeswell, 114
Beccles, Suff. 36, 38, 51, 142
Beckhythe, 77, 138, 140
Bee, 75
Benacre, Suff. 110
Benham, Mary, 119
Benjamin, 101
Bennett, 57
Bergen, North 29
Berwick, 89
Bevan, Thomas, 72
Billockby, 113
Billop, Captain, 30
Bixley, 151
Black Shuck, 153
Blade, James, 34
Blake, Edward, 96
Blakeney, 11, 25, 29, 56, 78, 89, 90, 92,

116, 117, 129, 151
Bliss, Mr, 55, 56
Bodney Warren, 148, 150
Boston, Lincs. 30, 31, 51, 75, 99, 104
Boulogne, France,72, 109
Bowles, Capt. William 105
Bowring, John, 133
Boyles, Mr, 37
Bramerton, 38, 142, 143
Bramford, Suff. 151
Brancaster, 16, 25, 28, 43, 75, 104, 164
Bremen, Germany 83
Brett, Nannie, 158
Breydon Water, 95, 161
Bridden, Mr, 60
Bridge, Cyprian, 74,
Brisk, 93
Briston, 152
Brock, Mr, 51
Broke, John 14
Bromholm, 12
Brookes, Thomas, 38
Bruges, Belgium, 14, 95
Buck, Mr, 79
Buck, John,125
Buck, John, 162
Buller, Judge Francis, 147
Bungay, Suff. 51, 120
Burchett, Josiah, 27
Bure, River, 96, 140, 143, 144, 145, 146
Burlingham, 49
Burnham Deepdale, 60
Burnham Market, 130
Burnham Sutton, 130
Burton, brothers 130
Butcher, Mark, 119, 120, 121
Butler, George, 25
Buttlesly Green, Suff. 39
Buxton, 55,
Buxton, Sarah,138
Caister, 60, 102, 113
Calais, France, 14, 16, 32, 97, 109
Cambridge, Cambs. 37
Carbold, James, 38, 143
Carman, 102

Castle Rising, 12, 13
Cawston, 55, 85, 86, 114, 115
Challiner, Francis, 25
Chatham, Kent, 10, 100
Cherbourg, France, 107
Christmas, Samuel, 147
Church, William, 28-9
Churchman,Thomas, 63
Clark, Robert, 37
Clarke, James, 40
Clarke, Thomas, 24
Claxton, 147
Claxton, Lieut. 99
Cley, 25, 29, 39, 56, 59, 89, 90, 129, 135
Coates, Henry, 147
Cock, Charles, 61
Cock, Thomas 147
Colby, 139
Colby, Mr, 113
Colchester, Essex, 109, 148
Collings, Godfrey, 42
Coltishall, 55
Constant Friends, 74
Cossack, 98
Cousins, Thomas, 82
Cox, Henry, 19
Cox, Gabriell, 25
Cringleford, 65, 151
Croft, John, alias Meyer, 15, 16
Cromer, 16, 26, 29, 49, 55, 74, 75, 78,
    100, 114, 118, 128, 135, 165
Cruizer, 84
Cubitt, Revd John, 126
Culley, William, 155, 156
Cunningham, John, 38
Cunningham, Robert, 37, 38
Cunningham, William, 38
Custin, Samuel, 110
Cutting, Mr, 137
Daniel, Robert, 18
Daniel, Peter, 83
Darby, Daniel, 24, 25, 27
Darby, William, 138
Dashwood, Samuel, 21
Davey, John, 82
De Hoop, 95, 98
De Lafosse, Capt. 121
Deal, Kent, 85, 87, 97
Deception, 76
Deopham, 110
Diggens, Thomas, 47, 52
Diss, 35, 37, 38, 41, 43

Dobson, George, 102
Doe, John, 38, 143
Dover, Kent, 72, 97, 124
Downes, Richard, 18
Downham, 34
Duke of Wellington, 98
Dunkirk, France, 42, 73, 75, 97
Dunmow, 65
Dunwich, Suff. 133
Eager, Samuel, 37
Eager, Mrs, 62
Earsham, 119, 120, 121
East Dereham, 131
East Tuddenham, 162
Easton, 51
Easy, James, 133
Eccles, 151
Edge, Edmund, 25
Edgefield, 116, 160
Edinburgh, Scotland, 60
Elizabeth, 16
Ellingham, 113
Elliot, General, 57, 112
Ellis, Mr, 130
Elsinore, Denmark, 83
Ely, 38
Enton, Peter, 20
Erpingham, 54
Essex, 63, 73, 75, 150
Eyre, Baron, 119
Fall, Midshipman, 77
Fate, 164
Faulk,Thomas, 26-7
Fawsset, William, 111
Felbrigg, 72
Fenn, John, 147
Filby, 113
Fisher, Robert, 35, 41
Fisher, Capt. 76, 77, 81
Flanders, 14
Fleading, 13
Fleet Prison, 53
Flitcham, 42
Florida, 97
Flushing, Belgium, 73, 74, 76, 78, 79, 86,
    107, 108, 165
Fly, 76
Folkestone, Kent, 76
Folkestone, 99
Ford, Drury, 160
Fordham, Simon, 40
Forster, Peter, 125, 126

Foulsham, 114
Fox, 85, 110
Framingham, 28
France, 16, 27, 31, 51, 62, 78, 79, 85, 86,
    90, 124
Franklin, Thomas, 55, 56
Fritton, 129
Fry, Elizabeth, 108
Galloway, Tom, 38
Gedge, 65
Gee, Charles, 59, 77, 132
Gent, William, 25
George, 74
Georgie, The Little, 146-7
Getting, Edward, 25
Gimingham, 113
Godfrey, Owen, 25
Good Intent, 73
Gorleston, 27, 40, 163
Gotobed, J., 164
Gowen, Charles, 38, 143
Grapes Mill, 144
Gray, John, 140
Great Ouse, River, 18, 111
Great Snoring, 151
Great Yarmouth, 11, 13, 15, 16, 18, 20,
    24, 25, 26, 27, 28, 29, 30,31, 32, 37,
    38, 40, 41, 42, 44, 46, 49, 56, 59, 60,
    61, 63, 73, 76, 77, 78, 80, 81, 82, 83,
    84, 87, 88, 90, 93, 94, 95, 96, 97, 98,
    99, 100, 101, 102, 103, 104, 105, 108,
    110, 129, 130, 136, 138, 142,143, 144,
    146, 151, 161, 162, 165
Green, William, 57, 58, 59, 163
Greyhound, 51, 52
Griggs, Thomas, 43
Gunthorpe, Capt. 80, 81
Gunton, 57, 152
Gurney, Anna,138
Gybbeson, Simon, 13, 14
Hagon, Robert,142
Hale, Sir Matthew, 21
Hall, Mr, 47, 64, 72, 74, 139
Hamburg, Germany, 74
Hampshire, 85, 151
Hanworth Common, 150
Happisburgh, 16, 56, 73, 81, 83, 100,
    101, 130, 137, 144, 146, 153, 160, 165
Harbord, Sir H. 124
Hardy, 98
Harleston, 51, 152
Harold, Capt. Peter, 24, 31

Harriet, 107
Harrison, George, 37
Harwich, Essex, 32, 72, 73, 74, 75
Haslip, Mr, 50
Hawarden Castle, 166
Hawk, 98
Hawthyne, Capt. 97
Heacham, 25, 29, 112, 134
Hempnall, 37
Hempstead, 104, 113, 152
Hemsby, 16, 104, 136
Hevingham, 115
Hewitt, Clerk, 125
Heybeck, Jan, 96
Hickling, 126, 146, 151
Hoare, Sir Samuel, 138
Hockering, 51
Holland, 10, 15, 27, 32, 41, 51, 74, 134
Holt, 107, 114, 138, 154, 155, 160
Honingham, 125
Hope, 84
Hopgood, 102
Hornsby, Capt. 165
Horsey, 81, 142, 144, 146
Horstead, 144, 145
Houghton, 27
Howard, General, 39
Howe, 37
Howes, Lieut. 103, 104, 164
Hoxne, Suff. 39
Hoyle, Isaac, 43
Hull, Yorks. 58, 74, 165
Humber, River, 166
Hunstanton, 29, 51, 52, 55, 56, 57, 58,
    78, 107, 112, 134, 148
Hunter, 59, 77, 80, 81, 82, 83, 101, 138
Icknield Way, 148, 150
Ilford, Essex, 45
Industry, 98
Ipswich, Suff. 109, 110, 151
Isabella, Queen, 12, 13
Isle of Wight, 26
Ives, Alderman,
Jackson, John, 24 124
James and Polly, 74
Jay, Thomas, 59, 77, 83
Jenkins, 50
Jewel, Mr, 56
Jewell, 137
Johnson, John, 34
Johnson, Tom, 85
Kelling, 152, 164

Kemble, 57, 58, 132
Kenninghall, 152
Kent, 8, 26, 37, 50, 63, 85, 96, 154, 165
Kerrison, Sir Roger 127
Kessingland, 98, 147
Kimberley, 39
Kinch, George, 43
King's Bench Prison, 53, 127, 128
King's Lynn, 11, 12, 15, 16, 17, 18, 19,
    20, 23, 24, 25, 26, 28, 29, 42, 51, 52,
    55, 60, 68, 74, 78, 84, 111, 112, 130,
    164, 166
Kirke, Samuel, 25
Knapton, 12, 13
La Godirad, 13
La Leverette, 103
Lakenham, 37
Lamb, Mayor Thomas Philip, 64
Langham, 107
Lawrence, Edward, 24
Le Blanc, Mr Justice, 128
Lea, James, 147
Leeds, Yorks. 166
Lenwade, 125, 126
Lewes, Sussex, 43
Lewis, Charles, 24
Liberty, 77
Linder, 105
Lindsey, Suff.143
Linstead, William, 25
Lively, 80, 81
Liverpool, Lancs. 26, 83, 107
Lockwood, Mr, 59
Loftus, Major Charles, 159
London, 8, 17, 29, 32, 33, 36, 37, 38, 39,
    46, 49, 50, 52, 53, 60, 61, 65, 68, 72,
    78, 83, 89, 107, 112, 123, 124, 151
Lopham, 147
Loveday, Elias, 87
Lowestoft, Suff. 16, 76, 85, 101
Lowndes, William, 29
Luce, William,105
Ludham, 146
Lynn, see King's Lynn
Maasluys, 102
Mackarel, James, 127
Maidstone, Kent, 63, 64
Manchester, Lancs.166
Manners, Mr, 82-3
Manning, 127, 128
Mansell, Mr, 24, 148, 150
Manship, Henry, 18

Marcon, Revd W.H. 116, 118
Marryat, Capt. Frederick, 107
Martham, 144
Martin, 95, 102
Mary, 83, 151
Mattishall, 125
Mayton Bridge, 144, 145
McCulloch, Capt. William, 96
Melton, 152
Mermaid, 85
Meyer, John, 15, 16
Middelburg, Holland, 14, 15
Mileham, 34
Moore, Joseph, 150
Mordyth, Richard, 25
Morley, 33
Morse, Thomas, 25
Morston, 56, 93, 105, 135, 151
Mousehold Heath, 114, 115
Mullender, 102
Mundesley, 9, 12, 29, 32, 55, 89, 92, 121,
    137
Murphy, Mr, 58
Napoleon I, 85, 86
Nash, Richard, 26
Newcastle, Northum. 29, 30
Newgate Prison, 37, 50, 62, 112, 127,
    138, 151
Newhaven, Sussex, 96
Nichols, 56
Nieuwpoort, Belgium, 165
Nore, 10, 78
North Foreland, Kent, 26, 96
Northrepps, 118, 137, 138, 139, 140
North Walsham, 127, 151
Norwich, 8, 13, 14, 15, 18, 19, 20,
    21, 23, 24, 33, 34, 35, 36, 37, 38, 39,
    40, 41, 42, 43, 44, 45, 46, 47, 49, 52,
    53, 54, 55, 56, 57, 60, 61-71, 75, 77,
    78, 79, 80, 81, 84, 85, 86, 87, 89, 92,
    97, 98, 102, 109, 110, 114, 119, 123,
    124, 127, 128, 129, 131, 138, 139, 142,
    146, 147, 150, 161, 162, 163
Odiham, Hants. 151
Orford Haven, Suff. 83
Osborn, Robert, 37
Overstrand, 77, 92, 116, 135, 137, 138,
    154, 160
Owen, Mr, 19, 25
Page, George, 25
Pain, Ann, 41
Pain, William, 78

Paine, Thomas, 43, 44
Paine, John,129
Painter, John, 34
Pakefield, Suff. 76, 93, 147
Palgrave, William, 99
Palmer, John, 99
Papingay, Robert, 15
Parsons, Shylock, 127, 128, 132
Parsons, Richard, 38, 143
Paston, 12
Peddar's Way, 148
Pedley, Roger, 25
Pegge, William, 15
Pembroke, Lord, 53
Penrhyn, Wales,123
Perceval, Lieut.108
Persis, 101
Phillipo, Robert, 131
Phillips, brothers, 21, 131, 151,
Phillips, Revd Forbes,163
Pigle, 104
Pitcher, John, 59
Pitt, William the ygr, 54, 55, 70,
Pitt, 90
Playford, Mr, 118
Plumstead, 158
Poole, Dorset, 16
Poringland Heath, 65
Potter, J. 127, 128, 132
Potter Heigham, 144
Pratt, Jeremiah, 36
Prentice, Thomas, 21
Preston, John, 99
Price, Robert, 72
Prince of Wales, 165
Prosperous, 98
Pulham St Mary, 152
Punchard, Mr, 68
Pym, John, 21
Quincey, Thomas,137
Raby Castle, 107
Ramey, Mr, 37
Ranger, 98, 99, 100, 101, 102
Ranworth, 140, 142, 143
Raynham, 52
Raynor, Thomas, 37
Ready, Revd Henry, 126
Reepham, 43
Repulse, 85, 98, 104
Resolution, 84
Riches, Capt. Thomas, 82, 83
Ringstead, 152

Roads, Henry, 37
Robin Hood's Bay, Yorks. 99
Rochester, Kent, 73
Rook, John,129
Roscoff, France, 86, 107
Rose, William, 40, 41
Rotterdam, Holland, 73
Royal, Benjamin, 78
Royall, brothers, 161, 162
Rudd, Tom,146
Runham, 95, 146
Runton, 78, 114, 135, 136
Rye, Sussex, 64, 123
Saiffart, Andres, 96
Salisbury, Wilts. 16
Salthouse, 25, 90, 107
Sandby, Revd G., 119
Sanderson, Thomas, 43
Sandgate, Kent, 76
Sandringham, 122
Sarwood, John, 103
Saxmundham, Suff. 93
Sayer, John, 37
Sayers, Capt. John, 98, 99, 100, 101
Schiedam, Holland, 75, 154
Scottow, 68
Sea Flower, 165
Sea Palling, 37, 126, 133, 160
Seagull, 85
Sedgeford, 130
Setch, 152
Sharp, Capt. 124
Shaxton, Thomas, 18
Shelton, 110
Shepherd, 34
Sheringham, 54, 90, 135
Shipdham, 49
Shorten, Robert, 42
Shotesham, 60
Sidestrand, 116, 137, 160, 162
Sileham, Suff. 41
Silver, Billy, 139
Silvers, Brighton, 94, 95, 102, 146
Sizewell, Suff. 74
Skipstale, Philip,13
Smyth, William, 18
Sneller, James, 103
Snettisham, 35
South Walsham, 146
Southampton, Hants. 20
Southgate, John, 31,
Southgate, Capt. William, 42

Southrepps, 137, 152
Southwold, Suff. 50, 51, 82
Spencer, William, 55
St Faith's, Horsham, 15
St Omer, 14
St Petersburg, 107
St Thomas, 97
Stalham, 146, 152
Stanfield Green, 34
Stanford, 148, 150
Steward, Capt. Timothy, 70, 81
Stewart, 97, 142
Stiffkey, 159
Stockton, Durham,107
Stoddart,Capt. 84
Stokes, William,15
Suffield, 121
Suffolk, 8, 11, 32, 33, 36, 38, 41, 49, 50,
    51, 63, 73, 74, 75, 78, 80, 83, 93, 98,
    109, 110, 118, 121, 133, 143, 147, 150,
    151, 154
Suggett, William, 98
Summers, Ted, 138, 139
Surlingham, 140
Susannah, 100
Sussex, 43, 64, 96, 123, 165
Sustead, 142
Sutton, 146, 150
Swaffham, 148
Swanton, 27
Swanton Abbot, 131
Sydestrand, 92
Sydney,Thomas, 18
Symonds, George, 20
Tartar, 95, 98, 99, 101
Taylor, Mr, 130
Terrington Steep, 25, 26
Themelthorpe, 131
Thetford, 41, 43, 47, 50, 67, 148, 150
Thetford, Robert, 25
Thompson, Robert, 25
Thompson, James, 47
Thornham, 42, 51, 55, 90, 112, 134
Thorpe Market, 152
Three Brothers, 76
Thurkyld, Simon, 13
Thurne, River, 146
Thurston, John, 16
Tiger, 90
Tit, Tom, 37, 38
Titcomb, 83
Toby, Mr, 102

Toll, Robert, 27
Townsend, John, 25
Townshend, Lord, 47, 48, 55
Trimingham, 78, 79, 152
Trowse, 61, 151
Trunch, 152
van Burke, William, 16
Vere, Holland, 16
Vernon, Luke, 59
Volharden, 108
Waits, John, 43
Wake, John, 127
Waller, Robert, 98, 151
Walpole, Sir Robert, 6, 27-28
Walpole, 31
Walpole, Horatio Lord, 127
Walsham, Martin, 15
Walsingham, 18, 133
Ward, 104
Warham, 27, 93
Warner, William, 12, 13
Watt, Thomas, 83
Wattlefield, 33
Watts, Robert and Ireland,121
Waveney, River, 147
Waxham, 126
Wayman, Samuel, 37, 38
Webb, William, 57, 58
Webb,148
Weeks, 65
Wells-next-the-Sea, 25, 27, 29, 31, 41, 43,
    55, 58, 71, 74, 134, 136, 159, 164
Wensum, River, 67
Wesley, John, 124
West, Richard, 25
West Raynham, 47, 48
West Rudham, 152
Weston Longville, 70, 124
Weybourne, 92, 103, 117, 135, 152
Wigg, Charles, 99
Wigget, John, 20, 21
Wight, Richard, 25
Williams, Thomas, 57, 73, 133
Wilson, George, 16, 17
Wilson, John, 37
Wimbotsham, 34
Windham, William, 72, 124,
Windham, Charles, 127
Windsel, John, 83
Winterton, 103, 146
Wissey, River, 150
Witton, 114

Wolferton, 134
Wood, John, 25
Woodbastwick, 151
Woodbridge, Suff. 11, 74
Woodforde, Revd James, 70, 124, 125
Woodham, Richard, 98
Woodhouse, 102
Wootton, 111
Worthington, Capt. 101
Wright,Francis, 83
Wright, 102
Wroxham, 146
Wymondham, 33, 39, 133
Yare, River, 95, 142, 147, 161
Yaxley, Suff. 51
York, 34, 67
Yorkshire, 96, 99
Young, Robert, 38,